THE GARDENS OF CAMELOT

THE GARDENS
OF CAMELOT

By

Rupert Croft-Cooke

PUTNAM
42 GREAT RUSSELL STREET
LONDON MCMLVIII

Made and printed in Great Britain
by The Camelot Press Ltd, Southampton
for the publishers Putnam & Company Ltd

Contents

'I think that we
Shall never more, at any future time,
Delight our souls with talk of knightly deeds,
Walking about the gardens and the halls
Of Camelot, as in the days that were.'
                    The Passing of Arthur, TENNYSON

"It is not my own development which interests me now so much as the world about me, the people I knew and all that I remember of that other age. I want to write as people once did who had seen strange lands and come back to describe them to others who perforce had stayed at home. It would be wearisome, I think, to trace those years through chronologically, remembering this landmark and that in my progress towards maturity. I want to re-create not a sequence of events but a whole round epoch in a certain place and as it was experienced by certain people."

CHAPTER I

Two Victorian Families

[1]

IN HIS own family my paternal grandfather was known as 'the Emperor'. His tyranny was that of his time, unconscious or in his own belief benevolent, but it was tyranny of a kind almost unimaginable today.

He went daily from his home by horse-bus to the City, but his true life was begun when he returned to close the door of the best room in the house, which had been made into his study, and gave himself to his books. He was, I suppose, a learned man, at least he knew something of a great many subjects. Languages, words and names were his passion, and such was his blind and selfish autocracy that he indulged this at the expense of his children. His philological fancy was to give his sons Anglo-Saxon names and his daughters Greek ones. The sons were fairly lucky—Selwyn, Herbert and Hubert, but the daughters went through life as Agatha, Xenia and Eirene, the last named having Alithia and Georgina added.

'The Emperor says' was a fearful whisper among his six children, and my aunts to the end of their lives talked of his sternness and repeated sentences of his which ruled their childhood. If they were found playing with toys, or reading story books, his reproofs were certain.

'What rubbish is this?' he would ask. 'Why do you not study something useful?'

The 'do you not' in the question is a literal transcription of my grandfather's speech. He would have choked before 'don't you', won't you', 'shan't I', passed his lips.

He belonged to a time when a man's fads and habits were his rights, and of real moment both to himself and those near him. 'The Emperor is reading,' 'The Emperor said we must not,' 'The Emperor will be cross' were the scared whispers of his children, or warnings of his wife. And while these were being exchanged in the passages or dull dining-room of his house, the Emperor himself would be shut in his study, reading, perhaps, or indulging his taste for languages, uninterrupted and revered. He would emerge for meals, and while his children sat round the table he would question them in French or Latin about their occupations that morning, or reprove them in Greek for a hurried toilet.

'*Melines onukes*!' he would say to one whose fingernails needed scrubbing, and I have heard my father, remembering the phrase from his childhood long after all the rest of his Greek was forgotten, use it to indicate secretly to me that he had noticed the same lack of cleanliness in a waiter or a fellow train passenger.

As soon as the meal was over the Emperor would return to his own room, to his microscope and fossils, his history books and *Encyclopaedia Britannica*, and pass the afternoon in the eternal amusement of study.

As his children grew older he showed no sign of relaxing the rigour of his rule. Years after his death I was examining some books belonging to my maiden Aunt Eirene, and remarked that the fly-leaf had been torn from a well-bound edition of Keats. My Aunt Eirene smiled, a little wistfully.

'That was the Emperor, dear,' she said. 'The book was given me by a gentleman we met in a hotel, and he had inscribed it to me, a little fondly perhaps. I can remember how angry the Emperor was when he saw it. "What is this rubbish?" he asked, and tore the leaf out.'

Later still, when my father and mother were to be married the Emperor imagined some slight in that he had not been

consulted persuasively enough about the date. An invitation
was sent to him, but was returned to my mother's parents
with the word 'Cancelled' written across it in strong letters.
This was, of course, ignored, but he neither attended the
wedding nor allowed his family to do so, and my mother
still remembers his two then surviving daughters, my Aunts
Eirene and Xenia, coming tearfully to Waterloo Station
after it was over to see them off on their honeymoon, heartbroken at having missed the wedding of their favourite
younger brother.

The results of this despotism were discernible in his
children. My father was a rebel in his childhood and became
economically independent very early, but for the other five
the Emperor's oppression in youth was disastrous. My
Uncle Selwyn, coached mercilessly by his father, made a
brilliant start at Oxford, where he was a Hebrew scholar of
such parts that he was nicknamed 'the Rabbi'. He took
Orders, but was satisfied to squander his talents by remaining for all his professional life the Vicar of a tiny parish,
that of Belbroughton in Worcestershire, a rich living in the
gift of his College. He spent his last years, and died, in a
mental home.

My Uncle Herbert went into insurance, but was never
referred to by my father except as 'that scoundrel'. My Aunt
Agatha, 'the best of them all' my father used to say, was
killed in a traffic accident before the internal combustion
engine arrived, being thrown from a hansom cab with which
the horse had bolted. My Aunt Eirene, poor, amiable soul,
would have made a good wife and mother, but was kept by
'the Emperor' as that one daughter of most Victorian
families who remained at home 'to look after her parents',
and became a sex-starved old woman before her time. It was
perhaps my Aunt Xenia who showed most vividly the
effects of an unnatural upbringing. Vain and simpering,
she was married two years before his death to a rich old man

and lived to be over ninety on the proceeds. She was an evil-minded and malicious old woman, fawned on by the more acquisitive of the younger generation, and she died in selfishness, venom and squalor.

My grandfather's origin was obscure. He was one of two brothers, reputedly sons of an Essex coach-builder. But there was a romantic old friend of the family, an impecunious spinster who must have been a great reader of the sentimental novels of those days, who whispered excitedly about this. 'There is a bar sinister somewhere, my dear; you may be quite sure of that,' she said to my mother once. But when I recall that her hushed greeting to my aunts in their young womanhood was 'Any *beaux* on the *tapis*, dear?' I think it will be seen that her theories are not very reliable.

My grandfather was a civil servant, occupying a post at the Law Courts, the nature of which I have never been able to determine. The romantic old lady who was interested in '*beaux* on the *tapis*' lent colour to her theory about my grandfather's origin by pointing out that he had enjoyed the friendship and patronage of a certain Baron Pollock. My father used to recall that there was a major crisis in the family when this Baron Pollock died just a fortnight before he was to have appointed 'the Emperor' to a most lucrative post.

But my grandfather was afterwards given a position which carried with it a satisfactory salary, and entailed practically no work at all. He was made Re-count. The office was abolished at his death, and very nearly during his lifetime, for when the Radical Press in the 'eighties or 'nineties discovered that the country was paying my grandfather four hundred pounds a year, in addition to his salary as a civil servant, for the sole duty of being prepared to supervise the recounting of votes if the totals of two candidates at an election came within a score of one another, they raised an outcry which lasted for several weeks, and caused my grandfather to speak very acrimoniously in several languages on the subject of 'vulgar newspapers'. However, he held the position for upwards of twenty years, and during that time was only called upon once to fulfil its obligations.

Such a post, and his work at the Law Courts, admirably suited my grandfather's tastes, which were for study and travel. Every year he would leave his family in England, and, dressed in a long black travelling-cape and carrying a Gladstone bag, he would depart for a stay of a month or two on the Continent. He visited most European countries, including Iceland, from which place he brought home and afterwards gave to me a piece of black bread of extraordinary heaviness. His family viewed his departure not without relief, for it was pleasant for them to relax a little from the study of Greek and Scripture or, in the case of the girls, needlework of a strictly utilitarian character.

It does not seem that his travel and study ever produced anything, or were intended to produce anything except his own personal gratification. He read, and loved languages, wholly to amuse himself. No article of his was ever published or, to the knowledge of his children, written. He left no note-books. He did no research. Words were his hobby, and his hobby was a matter for himself.

'I have never read a novel in my life,' he informed my mother with severe pride when she remarked that his library had no works of fiction in it. That was probably true. Even the trio whose books at that time were most universally accepted as making 'improving reading'—Scott, Thackeray, Dickens—found no place on 'the Emperor's' crowded shelves.

Perhaps he was not a very profound man. He died before I was of an age to form any judgement about that. Perhaps his knowledge was too pecked and widely derived to be scholarly in the best sense. He left behind him a microscope with a collection of slides of his own making, the naming of which covered such a diversity of subjects that one must believe him to have been something of an encyclopaedia—though of how reliable a nature it is hard to say. But at least he was sincere in his love of learning, and there was no pose and no parade in it.

When I knew him he was in his seventies, a dignified old man who lived in a quiet house on Bramley Hill in Croydon. His study was at the back of the house, and had french windows which overlooked a pleasant garden in which there was a large mulberry tree. When my father or my mother took me over to see him I was always sent in alone to this study, which smelt of teak and leather-bound books and good Victorian mahogany furniture. And when 'the Emperor' had given me *chocolat* or a Chinese *higo*, and translated my name into two or three languages, he would take me out into this quiet garden, and if the mulberries were ripe we would eat them before he told me the names of certain flowers and butterflies and birds in Latin.

'If I had to bring up another family,' he informed my mother, 'I should allow them more latitude.' And certainly, judging by his treatment of the grandchildren, this would seem to be the truth. There is no fear, and only a little awe, in my recollection of him.

He was the only link I have had with another age. Born before Victoria came to the throne, he stands in my mind for all I have known of her era. With his wide, loose knot of bright red tie over the high-buttoning waistcoat and his check trousers, with his silver beard and thick silver-white hair, he appeared to have little kinship even with the period in which I knew him—the decade or so between the old Queen's death and the outbreak of the Great War.

He died, perhaps fortunately, before his standards had been quite destroyed or his quiet, selfish and dignified life interrupted. Aeroplanes and motor cars he saw, but it was his habit to ignore them. When his wife and daughter, walking with him on Redhill Common in the first days of motoring, called his attention to a horseless carriage miraculously following its red flag up the road, he reproved them for their interest in such 'vulgar nonsense', and to the end of his life he remained deliberately blind to such things, crossing the road in front of them as though their speed of approach was that of a hansom cab, so that their brakes screamed and their drivers cursed him. He was never, I am glad to feel, subjected to any of the indignities and humiliations of modern life, never forced to endure the cacophony of a thumping wireless set in a neighbour's room, never shot in and out of the trains or up and down the staircases of the Underground, never fed on tinned and frozen and chilled and medicated and desiccated and preserved foods, never expected to drink the chemicalised swill which the present-day brewer calls beer, never asked to make his visits to the Continent by aeroplane or into the English countryside in one of a halting procession of mass-produced motor cars, never exposed to an air-raid or to the impudent criteria of modern youth. He died while a man had still the privilege of deciding for himself how he would live.

A terrible and remote father he must have been, yet I remember him only as a kindly old man who gave me preserved figs and insisted that I should ask for them in Spanish and French before they were produced.

'Would you like an *higo*, my little Rupprecht?' he used to say. 'Would you like some *chocolat*?'

I can see him very clearly, standing on the hearth-rug of his book-lined room, wearing always the same attire, a venerable rather than a fearful man.

'Do not say "a blackbird", my little Ruperto; say "a *merle*".' I remember him telling me when I was showing him my collection of bird's eggs.

'His name is Dick during the week, but Ricardo on

Sunday,' he used to say of a fat old fox terrier who lay puffing near his feet.

'Never let me hear you say "under the circumstances", Rupertito. *In* the circumstances, my boy. Latin—*circum*. Things that stand around. How can it be *under* the circumstances?'

Apart from his study, his home as I recollect it was a somewhat gloomy one. A grey Croydon street, a house with lace curtains and heavy furniture, tea at an immense dining-room table, plush Turkey carpets and dark prints everywhere. Yet he in memory is not grim or morose, for there was a sort of twinkling kindness in his lofty pedantry. He had chosen my Christian name and I was supposed to be his favourite grandson. In an awed way, I was fond of him and cried long and bitterly when in my seventh year and his eightieth he died.

[2]

'The Emperor', whose name, I should have stated, was Edwin Cooke, had married the eldest daughter of a very large family. A doctor of some brilliance whose name I believe is still known to St. Thomas's as the inventor of the Croft splint, a certain Charles Ilderton Croft, had died in his early forties, leaving his widow with fourteen growing children. As usual with middle-class children who have early rigours and economies and struggles, they all 'turned out well' in a phrase of the time, and indeed several of them distinguished themselves in minor ways. One of them became Senior Science Master at Winchester and must have held the position for almost half a century, since I can remember him retiring when I had reached manhood, and I know that Lord Alfred Douglas, who died in his seventies in 1940, used to call him 'Old Crafty' when he was a

Wykhamist. Another became Managing Director of Charrington's Brewery, another a successful Leeds doctor, another, who was called Septimus, secured a place in a still more notable category, his name actually appearing in *The Times* under the heading of 'Wills and Bequests', for after a lifetime spent on the London Stock Exchange he left (to his very nearest relatives, I should make clear) some £100,000. The youngest brother, Octavius, was the least successful and respected of all, so that I was never surprised when I was found to resemble him. '*Isn't* he like his great-uncle Oc?' my aunts used to murmur apprehensively when I was a small boy.

The eldest daughter of this tribe, it may well be understood, had been an assistant mother to them, and no sooner was Octavius, the last, off her hands than she met and married 'the Emperor', some time in the late sixties of the last century, and began to bring up another family, her own. She was, I know, a gentle, practical soul, skilled in small economies, she must have spent the best part of her married life in pacifying 'the Emperor' when the children had upset him, or in justifying his decrees to them. She was a *hausfrau* of the old school who could handle shopkeepers as no women of this more tolerant age would dare, so that her children thrived, however small might be her housekeeping allowance after her husband had pigeon-holed his Continental travelling expenses and the cost of adding to his library. She was a most beautiful young woman when he married her, as I have gathered from a faded miniature, and I remember her as a friendly old lady who gave me tin soldiers and died when I was six years old.

Such was the family from which my father came. Honest, middling, bourgeois stock, you will observe. People who, if they died even in what were considered 'comfortable circumstances', had worked hard and economised long to secure them. People, I like to think, who, while never

achieving, or perhaps desiring, any particular celebrity or
public distinction, added their portion to the sum of human
effort as it was directed in their time—towards security,
consideration, the relief of suffering, the promotion of
British supremacy, and—more vaguely—the approach to
God. People who cared for and disciplined their children
and servants, were a little too conscious that they were
'ladies and gentlemen', but would have scorned to be mean,
cruel or dishonest. People who lived in hideous houses,
surrounded by grotesque furniture, who attended 'Eleven
O'clock Service', and ate a joint of beef on Sundays.

As I knew them, of course, they consisted of an old man
with middle-aged sons who had growing families, and
middle-aged daughters, one of whom lived with her father.
But by inference, by hearing stories of earlier days from
their survivors, and by recollection, I can piece together
enough of their life in childhood to imagine my father's
home. They lived always in what are now the outer suburbs
of London—Barnes or Staines, or, later, Croydon. They
must have had one of those gloomy-looking, grey houses
which are still to be seen in these places, with a small
garden, ponderous furniture and heavy lace curtains held
back by satin ribbons.

The boys were sent as day-boys to the London schools—
City of London, Christ's Hospital or, in my father's case,
St. Paul's. When they left school they started at once in the
City, travelling by horse-bus daily, as my grandfather did.
Yearly there would be the departure of 'the Emperor' for
places abroad, and their own removal to Brighton or East-
bourne or Hastings for a month of bathing-machines and
sand-castles. They must have been a close-knit family, for
both their quarrels and their friendships one with another
in later life have been passionate and enduring. Their private
idiom, too, persisted till all those six children had become
old men and women, and their nicknames, 'Shongy' and

'Tankie', they used till their deaths. They were for the most part sedate and industrious under the guidance of 'The Emperor', though my father was considered both impatient and mischievous. Their life was, even by contemporary standards, stuffy and over-cultivated, and they had no sense of the aesthetic. They were stiff, no doubt; they were rigidly proper; they were anxious not to be 'common'. They kept up appearances, and to do so they studied a rigorous economy. They were highly educated in the manner of their time, and thus supremely philistine. For a treat, my aunts have told me, they would be taken as small children to a confectioner's, placed in a line along the counter, and given a chocolate éclair apiece. Their tragedies were tearful half-hours over unlearnt collects or forgotten domestic duties. I do not suppose they ever went to a theatre, or had heard the names of their father's contemporaries, Swinburne and Thomas Hardy. But they were not dull, for within their own circle they had certain intensely imaginative recreations and secrecies. Their humour was esoteric, but abundant. Among themselves they had private games, private jokes, private stories. And it would have occurred to none of them to question 'the Emperor's' right to his own pursuits and indulgences.

[3]

This was a Victorian family, stern and rather more than usually Puritanical though its Puritanism was not so much religious as utilitarian. Pleasure was unproductive. Why read fiction when you could be learning something useful? The theatre was a waste of time and money. No one was musical, not one of 'the Emperor's' children could play any instrument, and the nearest they came to musical taste was a preference for certain hymn tunes. A stuffy, ugly life, and most of them remained stuffy people to the end of their lives.

It was a different kind of Victorianism which produced my mother, and it is remarkable to me and will seem incredible to those of a younger generation that such contrast could exist between the respective ways of living of two contemporary families in the same social and economical category. Here was the same philistinism, the same insistence on the social status of a professional family above 'trade' and below 'nobility', the same large brood of children, the same places of residence, the London suburbs, the same clannishness, yet the lives of the two families, their homes, their way of seeing and discussing things and they themselves were so dissimilar that they might have belonged to different ages and races.

One of my grandfathers was a civil servant, the other a doctor. Grandfather Cooke went to the Law Courts daily, Grandfather Taylor to his surgery in the City. One was bearded and somewhat severe in appearance, the other was bearded and bland. One had married the daughter of an impecunious doctor's widow, the other of a well-to-do barge-owner. One had a family of three boys and three girls, the other of four boys and three girls. One lived at Barnes, one at Highgate. Their homes, one would have supposed, were almost indistinguishable, but in fact were in strong, even violent, contrast.

My mother's father had a large City practice. He had started his career as a young surgeon in the Crimean War and had an up-to-dateness and enthusiasm for new movements quite beyond the scope of the studious 'Emperor'. He must have been what was called in those days an 'enlightened' man, for he brought up his children to learn things quite different from the Greek Testaments and needlework of 'the Emperor's' choosing. His eldest son, Herbert, he trained in medicine; his second, Edward, he sent to a German university to complete his education before starting in the City; his third, Horace, chose engineering, and was encouraged in the choice; while his fourth, Stanley, went to Cambridge and was called to the Bar. His daughters had exhaustive and expensive education in the subjects thought appropriate for girls at the period, so that my mother was a good pianist and my maternal aunts have painted, embroidered, raffia'd, needleworked, and even dabbled in pottery and sculpture. Besides these, the whole family learnt to ride and dance and play tennis, had countless friends and engagements as young people, discussed books and plays and possibly even socialism and economics in a gentle way.

Yet it was my mother's family which was the conventional one and, compared to its commonplaceness, my father's appears eccentric. The doctor's children studied artistic things because art was just then in fashion—whereas 'the Emperor's' children knew neither fashion nor art. My mother's four brothers were hearty, plodding men. Throughout my childhood I feared and disliked this quartet of cordial, athletic uncles, and in later years, in which they grew more and more successful in the most stereotyped way, I never learned to respect them. My mother's family was cultured, my father's imaginative. The pleasures of the doctor's children were everyone's pleasures—those of 'the Emperor's' were secretive and dearly bought, but passionate. The doctor's family was industrious, cheerful, sociable and successful. 'The Emperor's' had a touch of genius.

I remember the two homes of the last survivors of my grandparents' generation—on my father's side that of 'the Emperor' himself, on my mother's that of the doctor's widow—and they symbolise vividly this difference. The house on Bramley Hill, as we have seen, was all heavy mahogany and dark, plush curtains, low gas-jets on the landing, thick, dark Turkey carpets—a place of solidity and dim light. My maternal grandmother's house at Kingston had an equally hideous interior, but was light and airy, with a drawing-room full of frail ebony tables, dried pampas grass in pots, ornamental china, the watercolours of amateurs, and the sword carried by my grandfather in the Crimean War over the mantelpiece. There was a conservatory adjoining the house and several canaries trilled in it day-long. The garden had no mulberry tree to darken the house, but was full of flowers.

The respective unmarried daughters who lived at home and looked after their parents were contrasted, too. My Aunt Eirene looked as solid as the furniture about her and wore ugly clothes in subdued colours. My maternal Aunt Florence had pretty white hair, even as a young woman, dressed cleverly and to the end of her life had crazes for different forms of ornamental work in all of which she excelled. One year she would make hatpins and other objects from sealing-wax, another artificial flowers from cunningly arranged sea-shells. Once it was poker-work, once dyed feathers, once bookbinding, once raffia-work. She was 'artistic' and an Edwardian modern. But it was to my plain, heavily-clad Aunt Eirene that I went to hear stories which she made up as she told them—stories which enchanted me about good and bad children, and a character called Noodlums.

It is nearly half a century since these two homes ceased to exist, and the heavy furniture and rows of books of the one, the maple whatnots and work-tables of the other are scattered or destroyed, while all but two of those who lived in them are dead. But I can see them both as though the houses in Croydon and Kingston have remained miraculously unchanged, and I can still visit them. The last of my grandparents died before the First World War and my mother at ninety-three and her youngest brother at eighty-two are the sole survivors of the younger generation. I do not want to lament over those two homes—as well speak an elegy for the cave-dwellings of earliest man. But I am pleased and a little proud to know that I have seen and can so clearly remember another age. For the world of my grand-parents, it is scarcely necessary to say, was more different from the present than it was from the eighteenth century.

[4]

These two families grew aware of one another when the eldest son of the Taylors met the youngest son of the Cookes at the office in which both worked and the two became friends. But the families were never much more than aware of one another and have remained as distant through-out all their sixty years of connection.

My father, I have said, was the only one of 'the Em-peror's' children with the spirit to revolt against the old man's egotism. On leaving school, he was to become, by 'the Emperor's' decree, a clerk in the office of the theo-logical publisher, Septimus Rivington, a house which had been in the hands of one family since 1711, a house of tradition and immensely high repute. 'The Emperor' made it clear to my father that it would be a privilege for him to work for this fine old firm, and my father was duly inter-viewed by Septimus Rivington himself. What took place at that interview is unknown. Perhaps the great man was not impressed by my father, who appears in contemporary photographs as a slim, impulsive-looking youth, who wore the high collar and top hat of the period, and one of those graceful moustaches which grew untrained and unchecked along the upper lip and encircled the tips of the mouth. Perhaps my father was intimidated by so much tradition and theology. At all events to the displeasure of 'the Emperor' the interview which he had secured came to nothing and my father went instead to work for another Septimus, his mother's brother, Septimus Croft, of the firm of Marnham & Co., stockbrokers in the gilt-edged market.

This was considered by 'the Emperor' as an altogether inferior situation, for he professed to have no great opinion of his wife's family, and stocks and shares were clearly less refined and scholarly things than theological books. It was from this moment that 'the Emperor's' domination of my father lost its weight, for, although they remained erratically good friends till the old man's death twenty years later and although my father continued to live for some time after he went to work on the Stock Exchange in the dark stucco house at Barnes, he had now acted with independence, and held that independence dear.

Also employed by Marnham & Co. was Edward Taylor, my mother's eldest and dullest brother. It was these two who formed a friendship which lasted to my father's death. They must then have been as contrasted as the homes from which they came, for, apart from their different upbringing, they had highly dissimilar characters. My father was impatient and mercurial, his friend was steady and plodding; my father had been brought up in a home where pleasures were secretive and intense, his friend took sport and pleasure for granted. My father, after a frugal and austere boyhood, was inclined to be self-indulgent in the matter of good living, while Edward Taylor, whose home was a more prosperous and pleasurable one, had no repressions to escape.

Very soon my father grew tired of the pedestrian progress of a clerk in Marnham's office, and started to work on his own, but his friend preferred the security of dealing in gilt-edged stock, and stayed to earn his modest salary. At the age of twenty-four, having taken full advantage of the Kaffir boom, my father was making an income of £3,000 or

£4,000 a year, while his friend struggled for as many hundreds. But the contrast in the two men has another aspect, for my father's good fortune did not last—never lasted, in fact, in all its recurrences—so that his income varied barometrically from year to year, while the same Edward Taylor, who started in the office with him and remained content with his salary, grew slowly and progressively richer throughout his life. Thus, while my father died a very poor man, his friend had the satisfaction of dying a very rich one, which is as all moralists would have it.

I should like to have been present on the occasion of the first visit of each of these young men to the home of the other. What, I wonder, did 'the Emperor' and his practical wife and his two secretive, simpering daughters make of the young man who, although clearly their inferior intellectually, must have seemed to have a self-confidence and up-to-dateness which the studious Cookes wholly lacked. One imagines that 'the Emperor' found young Taylor shallow and chatty and retired to his study rather pointedly, while Eirene and Xenia probably held some whispered conversations afterwards in which their brother's friend was held to be worldly and modern, if not actually fast—unless conversation about his year at Heidelberg University recommended him to 'the Emperor' and he had the tact not to mention dancing, tennis or riding to the sisters.

The impact on the Taylor family of Edward's young friend, Hubert Cooke, was no less sharp, I think. By this time my father was making and enjoying a large income and had left the family home and taken a flat at Brighton. He was in his early twenties, full of gusto, not ostentatious, but a little proud of his own prosperity, and thrilled with his escape from the shadows of 'the Emperor's' dominion. He was already something of a gourmet and was forming a taste for simple, extravagant things which he indulged at intervals throughout his life. He already knew a great deal about clothes, wine, cigars and jewellery. His personal possessions as a bachelor, though few, were excellent—things of Morocco leather, gold, silver, tortoiseshell, whatever was considered desirable for a young man of the day. He was quite without knowledge of music or painting, and in reaction to his upbringing, in rebellion against those weary hours of the classics and history, he avoided books. (Indeed, to the end of his life my father scarcely read anything but his daily newspaper and *The Financial Times*.) But he had something which the pleasant and commonplace Taylors had not—that mysterious quality charm. That and high spirits and shamelessly open enjoyment of life.

They must have found him rather odd, I think. Something of a tycoon, he was in their eyes, but with the unwilling culture implanted by his father and his classical education at St. Paul's. They were modern, a little noisy, full of engagements, fond of dancing and the theatre—my father had been deprived of all such tastes and experiences, and his pleasures were more lonely and intense. But they must have liked him, for he was asked again and again to the house at Highgate.

Not many weeks after his first visit the Taylors realised that he came to see their sister, Lucy. But it was some months before the two were engaged. In the year 1896, when my father was twenty-five years old, they were married. My mother was six years older than her husband. 'Your mother was *considerably* older than your father,' my Aunt Xenia used venomously to say half a century later. They spent their honeymoon in Bournemouth, then settled in Brighton in a furnished flat.

[5]

So the romance of my parents was a thing of the 'nineties, but in nothing more than chronology. They were married in the year after Oscar Wilde was sent to prison and in the year before the Diamond Jubilee, but I doubt if either of them had ever heard of *The Yellow Book*, and, though both doubtless professed their affection for the old Queen and delighted as people did at that time in public events and ceremonies, they were totally unaware of the peculiar temperature of the age. The Naughty 'Nineties, if they meant anything to them, meant 'Ta-Ra-Ra-Boom-de-Ay' in a musical hall, not translations of Baudelaire and green carnations.

It was, I suppose, on the face of it as conventional a romance as you could wish to find, a prosperous young stockbroker marrying his friend's sister and honeymooning at Bournemouth. But no romance is conventional to its participants, and I expect my young parents felt as brave, original and in love as others who marry, as likely to succeed and as fortunate. They were justified in their optimism as events have proved, for their marriage lasted till my father's death forty years later and was almost unclouded.

I should like to have seen it, the ceremony itself and the reception, seen my volatile father while still a young, slim man and not as I have known him all my conscious life, tubby and energetic; seen my mother with those four gruesomely hearty brothers of hers and her two sisters. Most of the guests must have been 'friends of the bride', for 'the Emperor's' embargo on the occasion banned the Cookes, and though some Crofts appeared, and a good many Stock Exchange friends of my father's, it was a day for the cheery, stolid Taylors, who, of course, did this sort of thing extremely well.

I still have in my possession some of the wedding presents they received, notably a fine Georgian teapot from
my Great-uncle Septimus Croft, and most of the rest of
them were common objects to me throughout my boyhood.
What a collection! So typical of its time, so calculated to
show originality, yet so almost morbidly like every other
collection of wedding presents to a middle-class couple
marrying in the 'nineties. It was full of things that would
never be used, or be used only once or twice a year, perhaps—silver asparagus-servers, porcelain menu-holders,
plated oyster dishes, silver grape scissors, silver egg-cup
stands, and a peculiar quadruple piece of silverware the
purpose of which was to serve strawberries, sugar and cream
at one time. The doctor's gift to his daughter was a Collard
and Collard grand piano which remained with us for thirty
years through all our vicissitudes, though no other piece of
furniture survived the series of moves from place to place
which my parents' married life was destined to be.

The wedding was, of course, an occasion of morning
coats, high stiff collars, moustaches, and champagne. There
must have been sickening practical jokes by those four
cheery brothers of my mother and banal and jocular speeches
of congratulation, and a certain amount of relief, perhaps,
at the absence of the lofty 'Emperor' and his family. My
mother wore a fringe at that time and her wedding dress
was of white satin. (I remember finding it in an old leather
trunk in the attic of one of our homes twenty years later.)
It is more than sixty years ago—a wedding like a million
others in an age of early marriages and big families. I do not
suppose that a remark was exchanged which is not exchanged at every English wedding. I know that when the
couple had left for Bournemouth their families sighed with
relief, as families do, and said, 'Well, *that* went off all
right.'

[6]

I think I can picture the early married life of my parents pretty clearly. My father's prosperity persisted or increased, and after a while the young couple moved from Brighton to Horley, where my father rented a large house called Bayhorne. This, and the life in it, became something of a legend. There were horses and a coachman who had been in the service of the Prince Imperial and a smart little trap in which my father drove himself to the railway station each day and a dog-cart for my mother. There was a cook from a London restaurant and in the intervals of child-bearing my mother used to entertain quite impressively.

It was here, too, that my father made his first garden. It was a lavish affair, for he had large greenhouses and three gardeners. There was a great deal of bedding-out and potting-up, and flowers and vegetables brought to the house each day. A tennis lawn was laid, for another lifelong passion of my father's was formed—lawn-tennis as it was in his day, a social, amiable game rather than the earnest club and Wimbledon, professional and amateur, strained and disciplined affair that it has become.

So there he was, my young father, bowling along to the station, travelling with the same companions each morning, hilariously making money on the Stock Exchange—more than was good for him, it may seem—hurrying home to his wife and first children and garden, a delighted young man who never paused to consider his own good fortune.

In those years at Horley my two older brothers and sister were born at yearly intervals, all before the turn of the century. Encased in the manner of the time in frills and swan's-down, bonnets and ribbons, woollen vests and petticoats trimmed with lace, in sashes and pelisses ornamented with lamb's wool and heaven knows what other frippery, they were carried or wheeled into the garden and learned to toddle across the great, weedless lawns. The begonias, bedded out in patterns, were around them and the sound of the mowing-machine hummed through summer noons.

Visitors would see them and call them beautiful babies—their Taylor uncles in Norfolk jackets and knickerbockers, their Cooke aunts looking as heavily but less gracefully swathed as nuns, and jolly men of Stock Exchange acquaintance or old friends of my mother's from Highgate who were inclined to envy her her grand home and her happy, zestful husband and her easy births and healthy children.

It must have been a glorious epoch for my father, who made money with a kind of lighthearted brilliance which his seniors envied. He was a stockjobber now in the Kaffir Market, and I remember how years later, in speaking of the Kaffir boom, he said, 'I would not go down the steps of the House for less than £50 commission.' He was spending it as gaily. My mother has shown me some of the jewellery he brought down to give her during those years at Horley, and although it is conventional contemporary stuff—a diamond crescent brooch and amethyst and diamond rings—it must have been fabulously expensive by contemporary standards.

But, of course, it could not last. In 1899 the outbreak of the South African War brought a slump to the Kaffir Market, and my father, still under thirty years old, found the first of his little fortunes lost. Bayhorne had to be abandoned, almost the whole domestic staff dismissed, the contents of the house sold and a retreat made to far more modest surroundings. My mother was able to keep one nurse for the children, her Collard and Collard piano and her diamond crescent, but her new furniture went and was never, in such hideous grandeur, replaced. It was dramatic and sudden, but my mother was becoming accustomed to her mercurial husband, and my father insisted that they should both take it lightly. 'Soon make it again,' he said optimistically, and not for the last time.

CHAPTER II

Little Sunte

[1]

MY earliest recollection is of being held up by my nurse to open the door of a van in which the stag had been brought to Edenbridge to be hunted. This was by no means because my father had any connection with the hunt, since at this time we were passing through one of his most impecunious periods, and lived in a thatched cottage called Little Mousehurst.

My father's fortunes had vacillated considerably in the four or five years since he had left Horley. He had moved into a furnished flat at Brighton, and from there, with a slight recrudescence of prosperity, to a pleasant home called Haxted House at Edenbridge, in which I was born. A new decline had taken us to a white house at the top of River Hill, Sevenoaks, called Parkside, and it sometimes seems to me that I can remember a high bank of wet mould in which the roots of trees could be seen, and that with this dim glimpse goes the word 'Sevenoaks'. But the stag-hunt I recall quite clearly, the horses and hounds, and the deep voice of a man telling my nurse to lift me up so that I could release the stag. I was two years old at the time and the year was 1905.

The next recollection is, appropriately enough, of a move. We were 'in rooms' at a place called Lindfield in Sussex, waiting for our new home to be ready. I was sitting at a breakfast table and my nurse leaned over my shoulder to crack a boiled egg for me. There was laughter in the room, great happiness and novelty. We were to have a much nicer house, I knew.

It was ours for three years. It was called Little Sunte and was a former farmstead, now surrounded by new houses. From being alone in gentle pastoral country outside the village, it had become nudged by its neighbours in a row of recently built villas. But it kept its dignity and an acre of garden had been left around it. It was faced with old tiles of a beautiful quiet red, as are so many small Queen Anne houses in Sussex, and a few interior beams had been left visible by the builders. Its garden was walled and there were elm trees beyond it.

My father soon set about the task of making a garden out of the neglected ground round the house, for of all the long sequence of houses which he rented there was never one in which he was not determined to settle for the rest of his life. In these early days my mother may still have put some faith in his resolutions, for she had only had to move six times as yet, so that her long pilgrimage, with dust-sheets and pantechnicons, had scarcely begun. When my father found Little Sunte and told her about it she may not have learnt to foresee the day when the first warnings of an impending move were heard. 'It's a long journey to Town every day,' or 'I believe the drains are bad.' She may have believed that this was to be our home for many years.

Most certainly my father did. And as with every house he rented, he began at once to make a garden. More than twenty houses my father lived in during his forty odd years of married life, apart from intermediate furnished houses and flats. More than twenty times my mother heard those first ominous sentences, 'It's a long way to the station,' 'It's very noisy in this place,' and knew that a moving day was approaching. More than twenty times our furniture was packed and carried to another home, or stored while one was found. But not once was the new home taken without

c

my father's sure faith that it would be the last, the one in which he and my mother would remain to the end. And not once did my father leave it without having surrounded it with a garden.

Gardens were his passion. Several of 'the Emperor's' children had pent up in them during that stern upbringing a love of beauty in some form which would have been reproved as frivolous during their childhood. Only as they achieved freedom from the decrees of their father could it find expression. My father cared nothing for music, literature or art—but his garden was his pride. Twenty gardens he left scattered in the Home Counties, and sometimes I wonder whether he had not the creative artist's indifference to the thing once achieved; whether, having plotted and laid out his garden and seen the fulfilment of his plan in a year or two's growth, he did not become impatient for another piece of waste ground or a neglected desolation of weeds and broken rustic arches which he could restore to many-coloured life.

Not that he ever dug or hoed his ground. He had none of the tender patience of the specialist, who with consummate care plants each rare thing himself. He was far too eager for that. However impecunious, at any time he would find sufficient money for labour in his garden, and the succession of gardeners he employed is even longer than that of the houses he inhabited.

Before he left for the City in the morning he would eagerly discuss with his gardener the work of that day. As soon as he reached home in the evening he would hurry out to see how the men had 'got on', and would be disappointed or elated according to their seeming achievements. He had only just sufficient patience for gardening at all, for if it had taken any longer to grow things I believe he could scarcely have borne it.

So here, at Little Sunte, as soon as we had settled in, he

started to make his garden, and since we remained there for three years, it was, before we left it, rich and crowded and coloured. I can see it now—the perennials before the house, the tennis court at the side, the long kitchen garden with peaches growing on its farthest wall.

[2]

But of those three years I have no coherent recollection, no sense of the succession of events. In them I grew from the age of two to the age of five, and although there are episodes and vistas which remain clear-cut, it is as a child's uncertain dream, fitful and sunlit, that the whole time remains.

I remember waiting impatiently some bright autumn morning for the dew to dry so that I might run across the lawn. There were other places to play in, but the lawn with its drops and cobwebs of dew was forbidden because it would wet the feet and cause colds. '*Now* may I run across?' I pleaded till the shadows had passed from the grass and the lawn was dry.

I can remember sitting on the box seat of a carriage beside an old coachman who kept slapping my bare knees, and I can remember how, after I had gone to bed one night, I was dressed again and brought down because an itinerant photographer had presented himself, and all of us children were to be 'taken' sitting in a row on a garden seat.

I remember climbing out of bed at night to cross to the window and look at the stars. I have always had an almost unnatural love for them, and have spent cold hours staring up at them till their patterns have afterwards danced before my closed eyes. Nothing made me realise—when I went to South America fifteen years later—that I was 7,000 miles from home, until I looked up and saw the Southern Cross and the strange pattern of the stars in the Southern Hemisphere. As a child at Lindfield I climbed up to a window and was squatting on a wide ledge peering through glass at them when my mother found me and put me back to bed. But on other nights, and to my elders' apprehension on cold nights, too, I was found there again, always for the same reason.

'The stars! The stars!' I used to cry when I was pulled away. 'I want to look at the stars!'

[3]

The three people who dominated my life at that time were my father, my mother and my nurse. I can see my father and mother clearly enough, but I remember most my nurse. My father in his middle thirties had put on weight, and although it did not curb his energy or enjoyment of life, he was growing more solid in manner as well as girth.

I can see him in the white flannels and blazer of his weekend tennis parties, marking out the court. I can see him chatting with the gardener in the long kitchen garden behind the house. I can see him as he arrived at the front door in the evening carrying what used to be called a 'fish basket', a bag woven of reeds given by butchers and fishmongers in the City to those who purchased their joints to take home.

When he reached the front door I would run out from the nursery and ask for his cuff-paper, the little sheets of white paper supplied by the Stock Exchange to its members to fold over their starched cuffs and keep them clean for the day. Is there enough starched linen on the Stock Exchange today, I wonder, to make that supply necessary? The outer sheet of paper my father gave me would bear at the fold a little of the grime of London, and perhaps there would be figures scrawled on it. But within the sheaf would be white and inviting. I would scrawl on it or fold it into odd shapes. Cuff-paper—it is nearly half a century since I saw any, but it was the first thing I ever scribbled on (for I never had a slate), and I wish these words could be written on it.

I remember my father, too, when I was 'brought in' by my nurse to be inspected by visitors, for we were treated as children in the older manner, eating and living and playing in a nursery and taken to our parents when wanted. My father seems in those memories primarily a jolly man, but still rather remote. My mother is an even vaguer memory at this time. I remember chiefly that she wore a sparkling belt—what did they call that metallic stuff made to look like a sheet of minute diamonds which women used at that time? —and that it scratched when I hugged her.

But my nurse I really knew, loved, defied, obeyed and lived with. She was a remarkable woman. Her name was Patricia Spittals, and she was the daughter of a railwayman on the London, Brighton and South Coast Railway. She could read and write, but was otherwise uneducated. Yet her buoyant, imaginative nature triumphed over everything. She gave me so much of vision and perception and understanding that I owe to her memory a long debt of gratitude. She was so inventive and—ugly, but necessary word—so artistic that at the age of more than forty, when she had been with us for ten years, she set out for Canada and made a career for herself as an interior decorator.

I called her not Nanny or Nanna, but for some reason of my own Ninna, and Ninna she remained to me in letters across the Atlantic till a few years ago when she was killed in a traffic accident in London, Ontario. She was thin and tall, with sandy hair and prominent teeth. Inarticulately she loved all beautiful things, but especially natural scenery.

She would stand for long moments scanning a small valley or wooded hillside and tell me to look at a view.

'What *is* a view?' I asked.

'That's one, all over there,' Ninna replied, unable in her ecstasy to say more.

She never bored me, because she was not bored by me— at three or four years old, anyway—and her remarks on life and other people she did not keep to herself, but made aloud to me. This was a pleasant habit, and in retrospect I am grateful for it, though it would appear to have had some disadvantages at the time. Once, for instance, in that era of hats perched on a proud pile of hair, my nurse saw an approaching lady with a very mountain of chestnut curls on which a hat was poised precariously.

'I wonder,' my nurse whispered to me, 'how she keeps it on.'

It was clearly my duty to discover, so I marched straight up to the only person who could tell me, and stated frankly that my Ninna wanted to know how she kept her hat on. No record remains of the reply.

More embarrassing perhaps was the case of Miss Lancaster or Lanchester, an eccentric lady who wore virile, shabby clothes, short hair and glasses and spent her time painting in watercolours. She was called an artist in Sunte Avenue, though with what truth I do not know. She came one evening to show my mother a book of her sketches and I told her in ringing tones, 'My Ninna says you look like a tramp.'

'She's a toff, isn't she?' Ninna would say when a lady with the long white gloves, the button boots and the swishing skirt of the period passed the house. I would look out of the window to see what a 'toff' might be. Lesser, meaner-natured women than Ninna would have kept their comments to themselves. But Ninna talked to me as though there were no gulf between.

Scarcely less clear than Ninna in my memory is her old mother, who came occasionally from Croydon to visit her. Mrs. Spittals had few teeth, but the most excitingly fructiferous bonnets, and a habit of calling me Reuben, of which nothing would cure her. With her and Ninna I remember having my first picnic in the park, which stretched almost to the garden of Little Sunte itself in those days.

There are no more old ladies now, or old ladies as I remember them in childhood, who were not ashamed to wear bonnets and tippets ornamented with black sequins, and if one asks where they have gone one is told scornfully, 'But women don't need to wear such horrors now. They don't *get* old.' So the genus is extinct. But Mrs. Spittals was the best example I knew of it, and I remember her bonnets better than women's hats of last year.

Ninna was a strict Wesleyan and instilled into me a real fear of Hell, which, perhaps unfortunately, did not in any literal sense survive her régime. No doubt it was with a kindly intention of improving my conduct that she threatened me, in case I continued to be naughty, with an eternity of fire and devils. The fire and devils themselves were not very terrifying—if anything, they sounded novel and exciting. But I should be separated, I was told, for ever and ever from my father and mother, who, Ninna informed me loyally, would be in Heaven. This prospect so appalled me that I was found in tears at night by my mother, and Ninna was told to curb her ingenuity. This she seems to have done by explaining other aspects of her religion, for when my mother found me in bed one evening hugging my pillow instead of laying my head on it, I explained that I had been told to love Jesus, and I was pretending that my pillow was He.

Every day in the summer I was taken by Ninna for a walk, and these seem superbly eventful as I look back. Ninna had the trick of persuading me to this or that by the promise of a 'treat' the nature of which would later be divulged. She showed great ingenuity in the invention of treats, which might be anything from a crystallised cherry on the milk pudding to a peep down a well. One 'treat', before those walks, was that I was allowed to choose from a box of ribbons which one should be used as a bow round the silk blouse I wore.

What things happened on those walks! I remember halting to stare at bright red, white-spotted toadstools under a tree. One afternoon we had to take refuge in a shop because a bull had broken away and was trundling down the street. Once we were stopped by an elderly neighbour, a Mr. Varley, who was reputed (with what justice I do not know) to drink too much whisky. He stared at me long and I suppose mistily, then said, 'I see you belong to the No Hat Brigade,' and walked away The words uttered fifty years ago are audible to me now.

Ninna in summer used to like collecting what she called totty grass for the vases in the nursery, and I used to help her find it. But I remember, too, the agonising weariness of some of those walks, how I hung behind in the dusty road and felt that I should never catch up with Ninna, *never* catch up again, for she was so far ahead, and I was so tired that I wanted to lie down.

'Come along!' she would call, and I would make a spurt for a few yards. Home seemed infinitely distant. I was certain I should never get there. But somehow or other I got my hand into her white-cotton-gloved hand, and after that the weary distance was forgotten.

[4]

Motor cars were no longer a novelty in 1907, but for a family like mine, firmly rooted in the past and neither rich nor eagerly modern, a motor car belonging to a member of the family was still an exciting thing. One of my mother's four brothers, Herbert Taylor, was an officer in the Royal Army Medical Corps and came home on leave from the East to arrive at Little Sunte in a grey touring car. In this he proposed to take us to Seaford for the afternoon, so that my mother and my uncle's wife fixed grey motoring veils over their faces and my uncle pulled on a pair of terrifying goggles, and we started off. There was one hill, I remember, which was too much for this early example of automobile engineering, and we all had to get out and push it for a quarter of a mile or so till it reached the crest and chugged its way on. But I was old enough at four to feel likes and dislikes, and detested this uncle with his clipped speech and the woman doctor he had married, who liked to do what she called 'tease' children. So that the thrill of going in a motor car was damped by childish resentment.

I was, in any case, what was called a 'naughty boy', or a 'handful', and would howl with temper or disappointment so loudly in the garden that the next-door neighbours on one side of Little Sunte called me the Squawker. A tradesman at the back door one day alarmed my mother and Ninna by telling them quite truthfully that I was engaged in dancing on the cucumber frames. Shortly after this I took the bread-knife and picked up the cat with the intention of cutting her in half to study her interior, not with any malice towards the cat, whom I should have been ashamed to hurt, but from simple curiosity. My crimes reached a climax when I stole two ripe peaches from the wall— peaches which my father had proudly watched for a week or more as they approached maturity. After that my freedom was considered dangerous, and an ingenious device of Ninna's, consisting of a belt and rope, kept me in captivity as surely as a chain-led monkey.

I had my share of childish hatreds, and 'tramps' were the chief of them. I can remember sitting in the summer-house across the lawn transfixed with fear and detestation while a tramp made his way to the back door, expecting at every moment that he would see me and turn aside to drop me into his sack. I was not, however, in the least repelled by policemen, for my proudest boast lay in the fact that I alone had approached two policemen standing outside our house and asked them to show me their handcuffs. This they did, even slipping them on my wrists and off again, so that I had thereafter a claim to distinction which neither of my elder brothers could make. Time has, however, reversed this like and dislike, for I find tramps amiable and trust-worthy persons and have a contempt for policemen of which nothing is likely to rid me.

I fear I was not a modest or retiring child, for when asked my age would instantly and invariably reply in one breath— 'Three years old, and a man!' But at least I had begun to do things on my own impulses—strange and stupid things, perhaps, but of my own choosing. I was not, Ninna informed me, like other boys, who behaved nicely. I was 'always up to something'.

[5]

Not long ago, motoring in Sussex, I drove to Lindfield and with some difficulty found Sunte Avenue. Our house seemed little changed, but around it the whole area had been given over to the builder. The big house which had belonged to the mysterious Misses Catt was no longer visible and what had been 'the park' was a building estate.

Life must have changed entirely in Sunte Avenue, for its tenants probably do their own housework, unless they can bribe a 'daily woman' for an hour or two, bring up their own children, cultivate their own gardens and bolt their tinned food to crowd round the bilious eyestrain and boredom of a television screen. Most of them own motor cars, and few of them march out of their houses on Sunday morning in time to reach the parish church for 'Eleven O'clock Service', as we did, almost to a man. Conversation, manners, dress all have changed, not superficially, but in essentials, and the whole tempo of life has been accelerated.

Yet somehow I do not think that the tenants of those villas themselves are very different from the neighbours I remember. True, they are not acquainted with one another as we were, for propinquity is no longer a tie, but, allowing for changed appearances and habits, I think they are much the same. There was an elderly couple in those days called the Theobolds. The man had been Secretary of a London hospital and had retired to live for many years on a modest pension. He talked continuously and energetically in a flat, sharp voice, and my father called him Old Yap-yap, but liked him well. There were the Misses Waugh next door to us, the two somewhat acid maiden ladies who called me the Squawker, and on our other side Mr. Hammond and his daughter, Muriel. He was also on the Stock Exchange, and Muriel was a kind, buxom girl whom I adored. Then there was the artistic and eccentric Miss Lanchester and intemperate Mr. Varley. I dare say their prototypes still live in Sunte Avenue and entertain one another, as we did, to tea. I hope the children growing up there are as happy as I was.

[6]

When my mother was expecting her fifth baby and I was three and a half years old, I was taken to Kingston to stay with my maternal grandmother and my Aunt Florence, always known as Aunt Fo-Fo.

I have described her succession of addictions to the various arts and crafts of the time. There would be a smell of methylated spirits and burnt wood when my Aunt Fo-Fo took to poker-work, and after Christmas there would be in the drawing-room of every Taylor a table or a work-box or a desk with designs skilfully burnt into its light woodwork. There would be a smell of sealing-wax when she discovered a way of making brooches and ornamenting hat-pins by mingling into opalescent globes the colours of the waxes. Wool, leather, paper, silk were all mediums in which my Aunt Fo-Fo worked skilfully for varying periods. Raffia-work, rug-making, bookbinding—she did them all, and did them very much better than other women who had given years to one craft instead of the few months which she devoted before her butterfly mind had found a new way of making playing-card cases out of cigar-boxes, or of ornamenting hats with devices made from twisted straw or threaded leather.

My aunt's contemporaries delighted in her irresponsible gift of family gossip and supreme tactlessness. Later I was fond of her and learned to appreciate the unconscious humour of her outrageous family stories, but at the age when I went to stay with her and my grandmother, I found her sadly lacking in respect for my years. 'Three years old, and a man!' I used to say, but to my Aunt Fo-Fo I was just a quaint and naughty little boy. And since there is nothing more sensitive than the dignity of childhood, it took many years to obliterate the memory of her grown-up indifference to it. Still, it has taught me a lifetime's lesson to respect small children, who may have memories as unforgiving as mine.

My grandmother's house, with its mother-of-pearl work-boxes and little ebony, chintz-covered chairs, its sunny conservatory and remnants everywhere of the successive artistic enthusiasms of my aunt, would be regarded today as an example of Victorian bad taste. Yet I cannot help wondering whether the grandchildren of young couples who are furnishing now with the polished three-ply which masquerades as furniture, the shoddy little pieces 'suitable for modern flats', will find the taste of their elders so much better than the taste of our grandparents seems to us. That house of my grandmother's was neither beautiful nor very comfortable, but it had a certain character. However overcrowded with pedestal tables and framed photographs, with antimacassars and ornamental china, was the drawing-room, it had an air, it knew how to be a drawing-room. Will, I wonder, the toneless, distempered rooms of this generation, with their limed oak and their cream chair-covers, look anything at all when we are old? Will a chromium-jointed chair or a leather puff ever be regarded with the interest and awe with which I stared at the gilt bird-cages, and crowded china-cabinets, and huge strings of beads sent home from the East, which ornamented the house in Kingston?

I was not very happy there, I seem to remember, for my aunt was not 'good with children' and my grandmother was very old and had to be treated with awe. My visit ended with drama.

One morning an errand boy arriving at the back door told the maid that he had found a silver-backed hair-brush on the lawn. Further search revealed a complete set of combs and brushes, and almost the entire contents of my aunt's and grandmother's jewellery boxes. I had taken the whole collection and flung them out of the window.

If I could remember actually doing this I might be able to attribute some motive to the act. All I can recall now are the consequences. Whatever Freudian explanation might be found for what I did, I cannot help feeling that it was—I can find of no better phrase—for fun. There was no malice in it, I am sure, no knowledge that I was disposing of precious and beloved things. The glitter and colour of jewels being thrown on to the lawn was probably enough. Had I not already danced on the cucumber frames and proposed to dissect the cat? I seemed to have a talent for inventing naughtiness.

My Aunt Fo-Fo took the matter seriously. I *was* a naughty boy. I was to wait until my father heard of this. And in the meantime another aunt and two cousins should be told what a naughty boy I was.

Down the road lived my mother's eldest sister, my Aunt Isobel, who had married her cousin, Hugh Shelbourne. There were four children of this marriage, and the two daughters, my cousins Edith and Freda, were already bloused and skirted hoydens with their hair up. To this house I was marched that afternoon, dragging behind the determined steps of my Aunt Fo-Fo. Into a drawing-room which at that hour of the mid-afternoon seemed unfriendly and unfamiliar, with lace curtains concealing it from the eyes of passers-by, I was taken, and on a high chair I was set while my Aunt Isobel and my two cousins were summoned.

I remember the occasion so vividly that it seems scarcely possible that the year was 1906. I remember that I was angry and ashamed, desperately uncomfortable and unhappy, but determined not to cry. I think that this was the first unhappiness of my life which I can clearly remember, the first recognisable time of misery. Doubtless I had fretted and howled from the cradle, but no occasion for it remains. I remember this; I remember its agony.

My Aunt Fo-Fo began her recital. She spoke as clearly as a prosecuting lawyer. Then she paused. And when my Aunt

Fo-Fo paused, my Aunt Isobel and my cousins Edith and Freda turned to stare incredulously or reproachfully at me. My Aunt Fo-Fo continued, and their eyes returned to her. But presently she paused again, and again I was fixed with those shocked stares. And so it continued, so it haunted my dreams for years afterwards, the story of my naughtiness and the stares. First a few sentences, then the eight eyes coming back to me. I could not forget it. I woke in the night many times as a child remembering it. I do not recall it now without a faint backwash of the old wretchedness.

None of them were deliberately unkind women, but they were too unimaginative to realise what pain they caused. They saw the naughtiness, the unbelievable naughtiness of a little boy who had thrown handfuls of jewellery prodigally into the garden, and grown-ups are always apt to measure the sins of children by their consequences to themselves. My Aunt Fo-Fo was angry, and my Aunt Isobel and her daughters sympathised with her. And I was not even crying, so everyone could see that I did not care at all.

Then came my return to Lindfield, with the guilt of that colossal naughtiness still overhanging me. My Aunt Fo-Fo took me up to London late one afternoon, and I remember climbing into a very black hansom with her and my father. I was frightened of London, frightened of the dark, smelly streets and yellow lights, the crowded people and the noise. And as soon as we were in the hansom my Aunt Fo-Fo began again to recite the story of my crime. This time there were no eyes to turn on me, but my father, coming fresh to a knowledge of my offence, could only pacify my aunt by expressing as much indignation as everyone else had done.

Though I was unaware of bearing any malice to my aunt for the misery of those days, I realise now that for a dozen years or more I felt wholly unconscious but deep resentment. And my two cousins, whom I did not see again till manhood, remained in my mind as two women who had stared at me in my misery, two pairs of eyes turned on me in every calculated pause of the long story.

When I reached Little Sunte I was scarcely even interested to hear that I had a younger brother.

[7]

As though they were a compensation for the miseries of my crime in Kingston, I remember as clearly the occasions when Florrie would play her mandoline. Florrie was a housemaid who was only a little more than four feet tall, a dark, bright-eyed girl from the village. And when my father and mother were away for the night she would be asked by Ninna to come to the nursery and entertain us. Then the fire would be built up and we would sit round it very expectantly. My two elder brothers were already at boarding schools, so Florrie's audience consisted of Ninna and myself. There would be a discussion between Ninna and Florrie as to what she should sing first, but presently she would take her piece of tortoiseshell, lay the mandoline across her knees, and with long-drawn, almost tearful sentiment, begin to sing:

> He stood in er bee-ewetiful mansion,
>   Sur-rounded by riches untold,
> And he gazed on er bee-ewetiful pick-tcher
>   In er bee-ewetiful frime of gold—
> The pi-ick-tcher was of a lidy . . .

Florrie was in no hurry to reach the refrain, but swooped from note to note mournfully. And we would sit spellbound by the wonder of it. At last she came to the climax:

> If those lips could only speak,
>   If those eyes could only see,
> If those bee-ewetiful golden ter-resses
>   Were there in real-it-ee!

If I could but take your hand
As I did when you took my nime,
But you're only a bee-ewetiful pick-tcher
In er bee-ewetiful golden frime.

'What's it mean, Ninna? Why was he so sad?'
'Because the lady in the picture was dead, dear.'
But Florrie soon continued her repertoire, and *Two Little Girls in Blue* and *My Old Dutch,* however maudlin, would cheer me up a little before we went to bed.

[8]

While I was staying with my grandmother and aunt at Kingston I was taken to church for the first time. Most of the Taylors lived in the area, clustering round my grandmother, and Edward Taylor, my father's friend who had married shortly after my father, was among them. It was for the christening of his second son, my Cousin Arnold, that the risk was taken of my behaviour in church.

When I returned to Lindfield I asked to be taken again, Church, with its music, costume, ornament and colour, must have been to a small boy in those days much what a first visit to the cinema is today. We heard so little music elsewhere, we saw so few ceremonies or parades. So I was marched down to the little church with a sharp steeple at Lindfield and stood on Sundays and was awed by the majesty of the occasion.

The Vicar, I remember, was a Mr. French, and he wore a large moustache and one of those curious shallow pie-dish hats which are so rarely seen now on clergymen's heads. Moreover, he rode a bicycle and had once dismounted and courteously wheeled his bicycle beside us as he talked to Ninna. He was not, for me, the attraction of Lindfield Parish

D

Church, for I cannot remember him in the large surplice and severe black stole which I feel sure he wore.

It was while standing in the front pew and gazing at the choir that for the first time I gave my whole heart to another human being. There was a chorister singing lustily whose face I can see today, a dark, mischievous-looking youth in his later teens. As I stared at him he looked back and without for a moment ceasing to sing deliberately winked to me. This, I expect, confused me and turned me scarlet, but captivated me entirely. I do not remember ever seeing my friend again, in or out of church. He remains nothing but a white surplice, a face and a wink of half a century ago.

[9]

Another year at least must have passed at Lindfield after my return from Kingston, for another boy, the last, was born to my mother almost on the anniversary of her fifth.

I was conveniently isolated from both sequences and have remained so ever since. First came two brothers and a sister with a year between each, then an interval of three years before I was born, then another interval of three years before these last two brothers. To those who belong to large families the importance of that isolation by difference in age will at once be obvious. In some respects I might almost have been an only son.

It was perhaps the arrival of my youngest brother which gave my father his excuse for a move. With servants, there were eleven of us under one roof, and Little Sunte was scarcely large enough. But it may have been for some quite other reason that we left Sussex and moved to the Surrey downs.

CHAPTER III

Wayside

[1]

OUR NEXT home was a house called Wayside in the village of Chipstead, and we remained in it for six years, until the outbreak of the First World War—our longest stay in one place.

Those years were the last of an epoch which did not conveniently end with the nineteenth century. One might hear talk then of aeroplanes and motor cars and socialism and the wonderful twentieth century, but in fact the fourteen years before the invasion of Belgium belonged far more to the last century than to this. And no place in England typified that time so well as a Surrey village, no household was—theoretically, at least—more characteristic of it than ours, the garden-surrounded home of a prosperous member of the London Stock Exchange. Whatever happens to the world during the rest of my life, my recollection of those six years before the Great War means this to me: that I have lived in, seen and in retrospect become fully aware of another age, another manner of life, which will not exist or be imitated again. Each decade may have its peculiar flavour and aspect, and we have gone through the threatening 'thirties, the feverish 'twenties, and the tragic 'teens of this century. But the real division, the clean cut, came with the First World War.

I do not wish by any means to eulogise it blindly. I realise that under the prosperity and contentment which it gave to families like mine there was acute suffering and want, there were shameful injustices—not only the individual ones which crop up in every age, but general ones—there was poverty everywhere, and even in our village I remember unshod children tricked out in cast-off clothing. But I believe it to have been, for me and my kind, the last age of peace which we shall know, perhaps the last period during which we could be reasonably sure of tomorrow. It is fashionable to say that it was a sleek era of money-bags and righteousness, that it was completely barren, while, despite the invidiousness and regimentation of the present time, we can see in it the embryo of something better for mankind. Yet for one who spent a most happy childhood in the warmth of Edwardian days their memory is poignant. To me the Surrey downs as once they were, the house in which we lived and the people I remember there are all that I am likely to know of security, and there is scarcely a rambler rose, a straw hat, a dog-cart or a drawing-room of that time which I do not remember now with nostalgia.

In those six years I grew from an assertive child of five to a preparatory schoolboy of eleven, from being unable to read or write to having a queer distorted hotch-potch of knowledge crammed into me in preparation for the Common Entrance Examination. But it is not my own development which interests me now so much as the world about me, the people I knew and all that I remember of that other age. I want to write as people once did who had seen strange lands and come back to describe them to others who perforce had stayed at home. It would be wearisome, I think, to trace those years through chronologically, remembering this landmark and that in my progress towards maturity. I want to re-create not a sequence of events, but a whole round epoch in a certain place and as it was experienced by certain people.

[2]

Our house was called Wayside. It had been built about ten years before and was perfectly suited to its surroundings —one of those pleasant houses vaguely Tudor in design, but essentially of its time. You may find them all over the Home Counties now—all over England for that matter, neither Victorian nor modern, but comfortable and cheerful, built of red brick with exterior beams and white plaster and dormer windows. The ambition of their architects seems to have been to make each a little different, but not too different, from other houses of their size and period. So that while one had a loggia, another had a little circular bay at one corner with a pointed roof like a miniature steeple.

Wayside was roughcast, set in a garden which was large enough to prevent the house being overlooked, and had diamond-paned windows. It stood back from the road with enough shrubs and small trees around it to give it a certain privacy. Planned before the days of motor cars, it had a single gate of oak palings and a path which twisted among shrubs to reach the house so that one looking over the gate could not see the front door.

But at first for me it was just a house to find my way about as I had found it at Little Sunte, and a garden to play in, for I was still a very small child in the charge of Ninna. My father was heroic and Olympian, my mother had nice clothes and scents, but Ninna was with me, Ninna could be appealed to in difficulties. I loved her more than anyone at that time.

She was an unselfish woman, I realise now, and a pleasant companion. She was the first to rush to the scene if one of us was hurt, and last to leave the sick-bed at night. She loved us with disinterested fullness, she scolded, forgave and rewarded us according to her conception of right and wrong, and she took a pride in our achievements which lasted to the end of her life.

I can see her very clearly as she appeared in those days on the rough, chalky roads behind the push-chair in which one of my younger brothers sat. She wore a large straw hat with a black velvet ribbon round it, and an armoury of hat-pins protruding from it. Her dress was of a white corded material with a belt at the waist in which a gold watch was hidden, suspended from her neck by a black cord, and she had high button boots. It was the conventional costume for a nurse of the period, and it suited her long, thin figure. I would see her, too, in the clothes in which she went home to Croydon to visit her mother on her 'day off', a dark green coat and skirt, and a hat ornamented with artificial cherries and grapes which my fingers coveted. She made her own clothes, and she made most of ours in childhood, from complicated paper patterns distributed with weekly magazines.

She was ingenious; she knew curious devices for our entertainment. A rainy day was rendered exciting because Ninna could take a piece of black material, cut a couple of eye-holes in it, stitch on an elastic band to go round the head, and present us each with a highwayman's mask. In the summer old red curtains and bean sticks would suffice to make a tent in which the heroes of Henty's novels could live again on the pampas, the Sudan, the prairies. The horror of drinking a whole glass of milk was defeated because Ninna would add a few drops of cochineal and give us, as a great treat, pink milk instead of white. At Christmas her contrivance knew no bounds. Cardboard cottages, snow-covered with cotton-wool, would be lit up with small candles round the nursery, and the whole room would resemble the back-cloth of a pantomime. In such inventions Ninna was indefatigable. She loved to entertain us, and in doing so she richly entertained herself.

Like most townspeople, she could never resist wild flowers, and my younger brother in the push-chair would return from his walks peeping out of a mass of spring blossoms or autumn boughs.

But there was nothing gushing about Ninna. She never fussed over us with love and kisses and baby talk, but expressed herself with the strictest reserve even in moments of enthusiasm. The food she loved best was cucumber steeped in vinegar, and when my father brought one in fresh from the frame for her supper she would guardedly admit that it was 'not so bad', but beyond that negative she never ventured.

Her highest delight was to take us for a picnic. Do children in Surrey still have picnics, I wonder, now that the woods and fields in which we went birds'-nesting are built over, and what remains of the downs is fenced and foot-pathed and protected by the Green Belt Scheme? I hope they contrive somehow to do so, for I have found nothing to match the thrill and wonder of those golden afternoons in King Edward's reign when Ninna decided that we should take our tea on to the downs.

One of them, I remember, ended in tragedy. We had a dog then, a beautiful brown-and-white collie called Bob. My father had brought it home as a puppy a year or two before, and given it to us all. Perhaps each of us felt that Bob was in reality his own, that a strong if secret under-standing existed between child and dog which meant that Bob was polite to others, but recognised this one alone as his friend and master. I know I felt that. I used to march round the garden with Bob on a chain, chattering freely to him. I used to try to ride on his back. He was a fierce dog with strangers, and had broken two chains to escape and fly at unfamiliar tradesmen. But with us children he was docile and affectionate. I loved him passionately.

When, that June day, Ninna announced that we were to

have a picnic, I asked at once if we might bring Bob. And as the picnic was to celebrate my birthday, which fell on Midsummer Eve, my request was granted. So after lunch we set out with Bob at our heels.

'Don't go too far ahead,' Ninna would call to me as she hurried up with her push-cart containing my younger brother and the tea.

We did not go over the stile and up the steep slope of short downland grass with its may trees and rabbit burrows, as we often did, but kept along the lower road for half a mile to a point where a rough track went up to the right and crossed the railway line. By this route we came out on to a stretch of the downs on which the grass was long and heavily scented with wild thyme. There were cowslips here, and dry little violets near the earth, and chalky hollows. The field was crowded with wild flowers and small, scrubby blackthorn bushes.

Then we looked for a 'nice spot'. It had to be free from prickles, and have enough shade to spread the tea in, and it had to command a 'view'. The place Ninna chose that day was a smooth plot under a hedge of nut trees and wild roses.

The sandwiches seemed to taste of wild thyme, so strong was the scent of it in our nostrils as we ate. There was a special cake for my birthday. We munched happily while Ninna, who had gathered a great bunch of marguerites, enjoyed the 'view'. The sun was still warm when we sat down, but Ninna said she did not like the look of certain black clouds.

There were biscuits for Bob. He was panting hard, and frothing a little at the corners of his big mouth, his heavy collie's coat being too thick for this midsummer weather. I caught a grasshopper, and watched it. I had scarcely believed that there were such things as grasshoppers; they had seemed as legendary as unicorns. But there it was leaping, after a period of meditation, among the grass stalks. I could see the green, shiny body and great, hooked legs. Suddenly I heard Ninna calling:

'Come along. There's going to be a storm.'

I had noticed that the sun had gone in. The hillside had grown curiously dark and still. Big, slate-grey clouds hung over us. And we had only just packed up the tea things when the first big drops of rain, like wet missiles thrown down at us, began to fall.

'Come along. Come along.'

We began to hurry down the hill. The rain was slashing down on us, and the horizon had grown quite dark, except when great flares of sheet lightning blazed across it. One of my younger brothers was crying quietly as he clung to the push-cart, and Ninna's straw hat was already shapeless. We crossed the railway line and scuttled on to the road. We were more than a mile from Wayside, and the storm was growing louder.

'We shall all be soaked to the skin!' said Ninna, as she held her head down and pushed on. 'Into bed every one of you when we get home.'

Suddenly, a quarter of a mile from the place where we had had our picnic, I stopped.

'Where is Bob?' I shouted.

He was nowhere in sight.

'Bob! Bob!'

We were all calling and whistling. We looked back among the sodden road by which we had come.

'May I go back for him?'

'No, dear. He'll come home. He knows his way.'

It was true that Bob had more than once gone hunting when we had been out, and had afterwards appeared at Wayside.

'Bob! Bob!' All the way home we shouted against the noise of the thunder, and kept turning back in the expectation of seeing him bounding after us. But he did not come. We made our way, bedraggled and rather frightened, up the hill to Wayside, and looked in his kennel to see if he had run ahead and reached home before us. He was not there.

True to her promise, Ninna soon had us all in bed with bowls of hot bread-and-milk. And we were asleep before the storm had passed over.

I woke very early and dressed. It was Midsummer's Day and the sun was soon up. I ran downstairs, and found the cook already starting her fire.

'Has Bob come home?' I asked, and she said there were no signs of him. He was not in his kennel or about the yard.

I ran down the road we had taken yesterday, calling as I went. The morning was bright and scented after the rain—I can still remember the early sunlight on the puddles. I followed the lower road, and reached the track which would lead up to the railway line. I expected Bob to come running up to me, and called him again and again. Then I came to the level crossing, and found him. He was lying beside the railway line, and at first I thought he was asleep. Then I saw that his tail had been cut clean away. I stooped down and touched him. He was stiff and cold. He had gone back to look for us and a train had struck him.

There was a farm at the foot of the slope, and I ran straight towards it. I do not know now why I went to a strange place, for I was not a child to talk readily to people I did not know. Perhaps I could not bear to keep the over-whelming tragedy to myself. I remember crying as I ran down the hill.

'My dog's been killed. On the railway line,' I told someone there.

I cannot remember to whom I spoke, or how I returned to Wayside. But the brown furry body without a tail, stiff to the touch, haunted me long afterwards. The fresh early morning, the rusty railway line, the solitude and the dead dog I have never forgotten.

[3]

From my parents' Olympia it was decreed that I was too old now for Ninna, whose hands were full in any case with my younger brothers, and that it was time I had a governess. My sister, who was three years older than I, would share lessons with me.

Our first governess was Miss Luff, who after a short time was considered 'too young'. She leaves only a vague recollection of herself, a fair-haired girl who showed us a photograph of her father in the uniform of a Major in the Army. But she was succeeded by Miss Wain and there is nothing indistinct in my memories of her, for I loved her.

She did not look like the governess most beloved of two critical children. She was older than most governesses—in her forties then, I dare say, a peaked and narrow-faced woman with sallow skin, dark eyes and trim, unfashionable clothes. But her charms were not for the many—her abilities were perhaps unperceived except by us.

She would not arrive—by train from Purley, where she lived—until nine o'clock in the morning, so that I spent the first two hours of the day in Ninna's care. There would be Force for breakfast, and perhaps another packet would be finished, so that I would watch Ninna take her scissors to cut out the quaint figure of 'Sunny Jim' with the pigtails and top-hat and tight red trousers which was on the side of the packet, and add it to the procession of 'Sunny Jims' already marching round the picture-rail of the nursery as fast as our Force was consumed. Then if it was a summer morning I would run out into the garden before Miss Wain arrived, and perhaps have time to speed down the asphalt on an early form of scooter, which was the general property of the family. Or if it rained I would peer out of the streaming windows and repeat 'Rain-rain-go-to-Spain', or look up at the sky to see if there was a large enough patch of blue to make a Dutchman's trousers—a sure sign that it would clear up. Or if there was snow on the ground I would brush the crumbs from the breakfast table and throw them from the window, then wait for the first brave robin, the eager sparrows and the greedy starlings to come down for them.

At last Miss Wain would come, and I would run into the hall to meet her, then follow her into the dining-room, which was used for lessons.

I suppose that these can have lasted no more than two hours or so, that the timeless age of sitting at the table, the eternity of sums and letters, stretched only from the arrival of Miss Wain till about eleven o'clock. Two days of hard writing now pass more swiftly. It seemed that I should never be done with copy-books, *Reading Without Tears*, *Jog-raphy*, and *Little Arthur's History of England*. Miss Wain was never impatient, never brusque, yet she was never for a moment to be put off, never to be drawn into irrelevant conversations.

But it was when our lessons were over and we went for a walk with Miss Wain that her great talent and charm were apparent. For Miss Wain would let us look for birds' nests, even suggesting that this close-knit length of hedge would as likely as not hold a hedge-sparrow's nest, or that that holly bush was worth looking into for a thrush's or a blackbird's. Certainly she insisted that in birds'-nesting we should never take more than one egg from a nest of three or four, and two from five or six. But she understood the urgency of the matter, and when we pointed out that we *must* go in such a direction today, as there was a hedge there along which we hadn't looked yet, she never seemed to doubt the necessity, and debated as seriously as we did the choice between one foot-path and another.

Then when the year had gone past the birds'-nesting months, Miss Wain realised at once that butterflies were the only really important things in the world, and that when we took our walks the butterfly nets which Ninna had made for us out of green gauze, bamboo sticks from the gardener's shed and pieces of wire were as necessary as boots, and much more necessary than hats. She could discuss with us the respective rarities of our specimens, and appeared to be no less pleased than we were over the capture of a purple emperor, or a white admiral. She was not tiresome or authoritative—she made no pretensions to entomological knowledge. She was with us in our search. She did not patronise.

When butterfly nets had to be left at home because the air was too cold for the survival of butterflies, when goloshes were worn, raincoats carried, and puddled foot-paths avoided, Miss Wain was at her best. For she made our sober walks through the village streets wonderful with stories. Such stories, Miss Wain told. Not silly stories about good children who were rewarded and bad children who met disaster. Not Bible stories about bearded persons in highly-coloured clothes such as we had seen in illustrated editions of the Old Testament. But the stories we wanted to hear, about smugglers and pirates and secret passages and treasure. Nor did her stories aim at any artificial climax, necessitating unwelcome developments of the plot. Her stories went on riotously from day to day, and took their way from our wishes.

'And will you make him be *caught* tomorrow, Miss Wain?' we would plead. 'Can they get a ship and find an island, Miss Wain?'

Miss Wain would say mysteriously that we should see what happened when she went on with the story tomorrow.

'Bet he's caught by the pirates and made to walk the plank and saved by another ship,' one of us would say.

'Bet he isn't. Bet he kills the pirate captain, and captures their treasure.'

And when Miss Wain continued with the story next day it would appear that by a strange coincidence we had both been right, for the hero was in fact captured and made to walk the plank—breathless moments those—but was fortunate enough to slip out of his bonds in the water, swim back to the ship, kill the pirate captain and get possession of the treasure.

Above all, Miss Wain never descended to that contemptible bartering of rewards for virtue which most grown ups used. 'If you're a good boy you shall have . . . ' I remember from other authorities, and 'Not if you're a naughty boy'. Miss Wain made no bargains. Punishments were concise, and carried out at once. Another line of copy because one was bad. An extra ten minutes of scales on the piano. She made the bounty of her narrative subject to no conditions of good behaviour. She never expected us to earn the glory of a new episode in the astonishing adventures of her heroes.

Dear Miss Wain. She left us after a year or so because I was to start learning Latin, in which she was unversed, and it seemed necessary that we should have a governess who lived in the house and took care of us in the afternoons as well as the mornings. She left us, and doubtless other, perhaps less appreciative, children learnt from her their alphabet and tables. We only saw her once more, I think— a memorable day on which my sister and I, wearing the respective uniforms of the schools to which we had then attained, went over to tea at her home in Purley, and were introduced to her father and sister, and taken for a ride on the top of a tram—Miss Wain, of course, understanding the absolute necessity of waiting for a tram on which the two front seats upstairs were vacant. And we stood up in front all the way back, and clutched the brass rail in front of us, and sang at the top of our voices, while Miss Wain sat with her sister behind us, and passed us bags of toffee, and never thought of interfering with our behaviour, even when the conductor came upstairs.

Perhaps she still lives in Purley, an old maiden lady who has fought the battle of the alphabet with a score of different allies, and made her patience a decisive factor in every victory. Perhaps she has told many other children the interminable story of the secret passage and the pirates' plunder. Or perhaps she is dead. Whatever her personal fate, her kind is gone. Nursery governesses, such as may still be found, have studied Madame Montessori's excellent methods, and know all about child psychology, and doubtless as educationalists are altogether superior to our Miss Wain. They would consider her stories dangerous panderings to the predatory instincts, her encouragement of birds'-nesting inhumane. But none of them, I know, leaves with her charges a memory more charming, an impress more truly good. None of them better understands the children she teaches in the only way in which children can be understood —as one of themselves. For she was young in heart.

[4]

When we had those morning walks with Miss Wain there would be little traffic in the Chipstead roads. The approach of a motor car was still a matter for comment, and for the most part we would see no more than a carriage or two, a horse-drawn delivery van, a milk-float or a brewer's dray on its way to the White Hart. We would march up the road towards the village, and almost the first house we would come to would be the village shop. Sometimes we would go in to buy something and stare at the two old brothers who kept it, one Mr. Philips, bearded and brusque, the other red-faced and expansive, neither very encouraging to children. But there were bottles of sweets and sometimes a display of toys in the window, and once a wooden sword in a sheath which I coveted for some days before my mother gave me the money with which to buy it. The shop had a nice smell of groceries and oil, soap and cheese and fruit.

Opposite lived a man called Barnard, mysteriously mechanical, who was summoned to Wayside to do repairs at times, and whose dark face I clearly remember. A few yards farther on there was a choice of roads. To the left we could turn past a cottage inhabited by a family whose name I remember was Peckham, and who advertised 'Teas, 6d.' on a board in the garden. Another fifty yards in this direction we should plunge into a narrow leafy lane with a high bank of moss and damp earth on one side, and a hedge on the other which enclosed the garden of a big grey house in which the Misses Skilton lived. I do not know who they were or what they looked like; I doubt if I ever knew or even saw them, but I remember their big grey house and their name, from which we christened this narrow way Skilton's Lane.

But more often we avoided that route, since it led out on the road to Coulsdon, and continued up our own village street. There would be the White Hart on our right, and a pleasant, beery smell wafting out from its open door across the road to us. Behind it lay another big house in which a bearded acquaintance of my father's called Mr. Cheeseman lived.

Then we reached the village pond, on which there were ducks swimming and on which in winter, when it was frozen, we would make a long slide. Up to the left then ran a road to the Rectory and the church; straight on went our favourite way past the Post Office to the big house called

Shabden, in which Sir Horace Marshall lived. It had an ugly
Victorian front, but between its wall and the road there was
a deep ditch full of dried leaves which, we always insisted,
was a dried moat. In this we liked to walk, making the
leaves swish and rustle round our legs as though we were
paddling in the shallows of a rough sea. We would turn to
the left and reach a goal of ours—the forge. We would lean
over the half-door and indulge in that immemorial joy of
children—watching the sparks fly.

There was a way past there up to the church green, at the
corner of which stood a small pond on which I once found
a moorhen's nest with six eggs in it. Or perhaps we would
turn on our tracks as far as the White Hart, where we would
branch left to accompany Miss Wain to the station. This
road went past a house in which lived a Mr. Rudolph, who
might be seen in short knickers carrying a pole, for he was a
Scoutmaster; then past the home of our friends the Free-
mans, who had a little boy of my age named Hughie—owner
of a toy motor car much envied. After that came a point of
great danger—not while we were with Miss Wain on the
way to the station, but as we returned from it alone. Some
people called Lloyd kept a bulldog, reputed to be fierce,
which had once barked and snuffled after us. Even my sister
was afraid of this Cerberus of a creature, which did not seem
like any dog we knew, but with its flattened face and protruding teeth was macabre and haunting. We tried to creep
past through a little copse opposite the house, or we walked
up the road whistling, but we were always glad to climb the
steep hill to the garden gate of Wayside.

The ladies we met on our walks wore lace collars with
whalebone in them, large hats, and were recognisable as
callers on my mother. We rarely met their husbands, for the
houses of Chipstead were inhabited almost entirely by
gentlemen who, in high collars and silk or bowler hats, had
made their way to the station in the morning and gone by

E

train to the City, to return at five, six or seven o'clock, according to their status, like plump rooks homing.

But to see the whole population of Chipstead as it was then—perhaps in a sense to see the whole population of England as it was then—it was necessary to go to church on a Sunday morning in summer.

Breakfast was scarcely over at Wayside when Ninna would begin her preparations, and continue until one after another of us was cleaned and combed, dressed in his best suit, armed with a large Prayer Book, and considered ready for church. Then my mother would come downstairs wearing black velvet, and looking very young and pleased with us. And we would march soberly up the village street, not even thinking of birds' nests or butterflies. We would pass others as the church bells became audible, and when we crossed the church green there would be groups moving from all directions towards the porch.

A Mr. Harvey was the Rector when we first came to Chipstead, an elderly man whose features are clear to me, but whose seemingly interminable sermons and passion for droning right through an endless rigmarole called the Litany are all else that I recall. But the lessons were read in a ripe, throaty voice by a Mr. Adams, who wore a surplice and a sort of Order round his neck on a coloured ribbon which marked him as a lay reader.

I can remember the smell of that church, the oak pews, the musty stone, and the women's scent. I can remember the shreds of banners captured in some ancient war and hung in the chancel. I can remember Mr. Harvey standing in the pulpit for hours—days, it seemed—while I fingered my unfamiliar white knickers, played with my Prayer Book, or turned over the coin which I had ready for the collection. The collection was the only part of the whole affair in which there was any real fun, and that was over after the brief moment in which I gripped the discreet bag, dropped in my penny, and handed it on to the brother or sister beside me. There might be a hymn I liked, but *Onward Christian So-o-oldjer-ers* and *We Plough the Fields and Scatter* came all too rarely.

Everyone came to Eleven O'clock Service. There was Sir Horace Marshall, a successful wholesale newsagent whom I had once heard my father describe as a 'most vulgar fellow', there were the Goads, whose sons were at Eton, the Trittons, and the Cochrans, who were considered the village aristocrats. There were the strictest distinctions among the worshippers, and the lower orders were expected to sit discreetly far down the aisle, and not embarrass their employers by recognition. The choir was full to overflowing, for the prospect of a 'treat' once a year was still sufficient in those days to induce small boys to dedicate many hours of their spare time throughout the year to practising hymns and psalms. Bellringers were willing and plentiful, and worshippers crowded the pews. It was a most important occasion.

The church festivals for us were three and, of course, we had no notion of their proportionate importance. There was Christmas Day, which was scarcely a church occasion at all, so rich were its hours at home, its presents and exciting food. But the church would be decorated for it, strings of ivy hanging down the pulpit and winding up the stem of the spread-eagle lectern at which Mr. Adams would read of the Nativity.

Then Easter with a particularly jolly, waltzy hymn:

Jesus Christ is risen today
A-a-a-a-a-le-e-lu-u-ya!

But that had been preceded by chocolate Easter eggs, which were really the point of the day.

The chief feast of our parish church was certainly the Harvest Festival. Then my father, who never came to church himself, would strip his cucumber frames and marrow beds and send us laden with outsize *Cucurbita*. The church looked like a huge fruit and vegetable stall, and Mr. Harvey would preach from among bunches of grapes and Mr. Adams would stand in a sea of tomatoes and pumpkins. The big moment of the Harvest Festival was, of course, when the organ went deep into the bass to start the hymn *We Plough the Fields and Scatter*. There was some point in going to church that day.

When the everlasting Sunday Morning Service was over and my mother had whispered to us not to forget anything, we would crowd out into the sunshine. Such was my relief that the constraint and boredom were done that I felt like racing down the hill. But no such thing was permissible. As soberly as we had come, we walked homeward while my mother chatted to a friend. The lower orders would disappear in the open as tactfully as they had remained in the back pews in church. All was decorum. Everyone knew his place, and none would have considered taking advantage of the fact that we had been worshipping the Most Humble to show any vulgar familiarity with his superiors.

CHAPTER IV

My Father

[1]

DURING THOSE years at Chipstead my father ceased to be remote and became the supreme arbiter in my life, a reality instead of a mere power. He must have been in his late thirties at that time, stout and energetic and not dissatisfied with himself and his world.

I do not know whether even by modern standards he could be called a snob, for he never paid any toadying attention to social distinctions, but he certainly discussed his neighbours in the contemporary manner. This one was 'common', those were 'quite respectable', another family was of 'very decent people'. He would never use his most abusive terms, 'like the lowest of the low' or 'awful vulgar people' for the true proletarians but bring them out in impatient contempt for the pretentious.

He was what is called a dynamic man. The mental energy he expended on the current affairs of his family life was prodigal. He could plan, advise, perceive for others as well as for himself. The small problems which complicate the business of living in a modern State disappeared before the driving onrush of his mind. Problems of landlords and tenants, testators and legatees, litigants, parents, shopkeepers, quarrelling relatives, he could solve with insight and dispatch.

'Now what you want to do. . . .' I can hear the words now and they introduced perfectly splendid advice. But the person to whom he was giving it, some timid woman friend of my mother's, perhaps, might not have asked for it and was not what she wanted to do at all. 'What you want to do. . . .' The phrase is typical of my father, spoken vigorously to almost anyone, well known to him or not. He was not an interfering or a self-opinionated man, but he could not help seeing clearly what should be done, and it would have been against his impetuous nature to repress his impulse to explain it. He was the kind of man whose advice was sought by everyone who knew him, and given perhaps a little too generously and emphatically to please them.

This gift of 'seeing the best way to go about things' was something more than common sense, more than shrewdness. It was intuition, even inspiration. But it was, in a sense, on a small scale. It was devoted wholly to the complications of daily life. He could tell you the best school for a delicate boy, where to buy tulip bulbs and bedsteads, how to decorate your house and what clauses to have in a lease, whether a man was to be trusted and how to invest your money, where to live and how to make a tennis court, what to tell your cook and how to save money, which joint to buy for a large family, and which doctor to summon. Even on the Stock Exchange, a clearing-house for such information, my father was known as a man to be consulted. Yet he had never been abroad for more than a brief holiday, his politics were a set of prejudices sweepingly applied, literature and philosophy were mere names to him and his world consisted of England, or at the most the British Empire, and beyond it a lot of foreign countries in which anything might happen.

For the forty years of his married life he managed entirely and almost alone our family affairs down to the smallest detail of purchase, for my mother soon recognised both his need and ability to do so. She never handled any sum of money greater than that necessary for the day.

'Let's see, Lucy. You've got the milkman to pay today,' my father would say at breakfast, 'and you're going to get some eggs. I'd better leave you a sovereign. I'll bring down a piece of veal for tomorrow.'

That meant that he would walk round Leadenhall Market to make his purchase, and I can see him as he looked over the stalls. He was known to most of the butchers, who would offer him this or that as though he were the head buyer from a large hotel and not the father of a family buying a single joint.

'What about that little piece over there?' my father would reply, choosing with extraordinary flair.

Then he would arrive home with his fish-basket and hand it to my mother.

'There are some scallops for tonight, dear, and a piece of silverside for tomorrow.'

Even my mother's hats and coats were bought by the two of them together, for my father had taste and my mother had come to rely on it.

I have seen him talk to gardeners, engage servants, interview headmasters, consult a *maître d'hôtel*, always with the brisk good humour of a man who knew what he wanted and what he ought to pay for it, but did not underrate the other man's value and importance. He could be persuasive and amiable or brusque, but he always seemed to get his own way without hurting anyone's feelings. He was not pompous or self-important, but if he was slighted or flouted he was relentless, and I cannot remember him ultimately vanquished in any of the minor tussles which inevitably cropped up in the life of a man of such vigour and determination. But usually he achieved by a kind of businesslike suavity all that he needed.

He was, if you like, intolerant. Never having given any very profound thought to the wider issues of life, he had fallen early into the acceptance of certain standards, and he

adhered inflexibly to these. They were the standards of his
class and calling; they were the standards which suited him
best—but of that he was unaware. They were Right. All
else was Wrong. Thus he was a Conservative, and Socialists
were automatically 'scoundrels', and 'traitors to their
country'. He was an honest man, and all who 'got into
debt' were blackguards. In his loyalty to his own world he
had evolved a vague religion—the love of his country.
'The country needs', 'bad for the country', 'do something
for your country', were all phrases of my father's long
before the First World War. And he would have been deeply
shocked if you had told him that 'the country', meant for
him an England that did not change, an England that pro-
vided large incomes for shareholders and dealers in shares,
an England which suited him. He would have been deeply
shocked, because he was not a selfish or small-minded
man, and honestly believed that such an England was for
the good of her people.

He believed what it suited him to believe, but he was
unaware of that, having in common with his contemporaries
the gift of self-persuasion. All through our childhood my
father's successive gardens were his only extravagance, and
there were times when the extravagance of them was serious,
almost menacing. Yet—'I'm making this garden for you
children,' he would say, and honestly believe it. If we had
told him that it was for his own satisfaction, he would have
wondered at both our ingratitude and our blindness.

He could see no point of view but his own, yet he was
truly generous. He gave to my mother and to us whatever
he had, and it cost him his security. He must have spent
£10,000 on our education over a period of twenty years,
and he died a poor man in consequence.

All these are facts about my father, yet I doubt if they
give any cogent picture of his impulsive, forceful, boisterous
personality. For that, I like to see him entertaining, as he

loved to do at Wayside, and in summer it was always that almost vanished thing a tennis party.

It would be on a Saturday, for sport of any kind on Sunday was still taboo, not so much for religious as for social reasons. It was thought a little fast and inconsiderate of others to break the peace of a Sunday afternoon with the bouncing and calls of tennis.

After breakfast in the nursery I would run out to the freshly-cut lawn to watch my father marking out the court. This task he trusted to no one else, and it was almost the only physical labour he performed in the garden. When the whitening was mixed to the right consistency, he would push the small wheeled marker along the already clear white lines with confidence and care. The top of the net would be whitewashed, too, the boxes of new balls brought down and the net lowered to the ground till the time came to adjust it.

Then my father would walk in and out of the house and round to the gardener's shed, and up to his bedroom as he remembered this or that which had to be prepared. My mother, who would be concerned with the kitchen, would hear his voice in the hall as I heard it for more than three decades calling to her:

'Lucy!'

My mother would come to him.

'Have those people sent that stuff?'

My mother, usually able by some occult intuition to understand such a question, might be puzzled by this.

'What people, dear? What stuff?'

My father would be thinking that his guests would be arriving presently, and there was so much to do before they came. He would be a little impatient.

'You know, dear. That stuff you asked me for. The woman wanted for cakes. Those people at Purley.'

'Oh yes. The almond essence. Yes; Watson's sent it up with the other things.'

Then my father would adopt the slightly conspiratorial air which was usual when he spoke of servants.

'How's she getting on?'

It would seem that we had one of the endless series of new cooks whose succeeding and contrasting characters and mannerisms baffled my mother.

'She's a bit of a muddler. But I think she may do.'

'She won't ruin the duck tonight?' A real anxiety would be in my father's voice.

'No, dear,' my mother would reassure him. 'Of course she won't.'

'She did the salmon all right? It looked a beautiful bit of salmon. Are you going to make the mayonnaise yourself?'

'Yes, dear. Now you go and look after the tennis court.'

'But I have to see about these things,' my father would retort anxiously. 'What about the claret cup?'

It would be my mother's turn to feel a little exasperation.

'Oh, Hubert dear, don't worry me,' she would say good-humouredly. 'I'll see to that.'

My father would stride out to the garden again and look at his watch. Still two hours before his guests were expected. He would tell the gardener to move a pile of cut grass and send me to pick up some toy left in the orchard.

'Someone might fall over it,' he would say. He had inherited a dozen such anxious and warning phrases from his mother, and while he was the most impetuous of men himself he seemed, for his use of them, to live under the shadow of sombre possibilities. 'Mind that wire. You'll put someone's eye out with it!' he would say. 'Don't play with that, dear. You might cut your finger.' And so on. We called it fussiness at the time, but my father was not in fact a fussy man. He moved and thought and spoke quickly, which perhaps accounted for his imaginative warnings.

Another half-hour would pass, and it would be time for him to change.

'Lucy!'

Again my mother would emerge.

'Where did you put my white flannels?'

'I told you, dear, they're in the airing cupboard.'

'I say, don't let that woman whip up the cream for the fruit salad, will you?'

'No, dear. Now, you go and change.'

My father, looking stout and rather florid in his white flannels, would come downstairs with his racquet. His thick, dark hair would be carefully brushed, his moustache was shorter now than in the days of his wedding photograph. He looked eager and busy.

'Lucy!' he would call again to my mother. 'What time did those people say they'd arrive?'

'What people, dear?'

'Those people you heard from yesterday.'

'Oh, the Barbers. They're coming at half-past eleven. Now I'm going up to dress.'

My father would return to the garden. Everything was remembered. That piece of salmon he had got at the Civil Service Stores last night looked excellent. Duck and green peas tonight. He had put out the whisky, and there would be lemonade all day. Tennis balls, deck-chairs under the trees—nothing was forgotten.

These were exhausting occasions for my father, but I think I understand his motives. He liked playing tennis. He liked people. He liked entertaining. He liked, perhaps, the boyish importance of being a host. But more than these he liked giving pleasure. He liked people about him to be happy. He was a generous man.

He was also young. When the first of his guests arrived he would hurry across to greet them with unaffected enthusiasm. No pose, no pretence, but keen, conventional, ebullient questioning. How had they travelled? How had they managed to get up from the station? And the Barbers—

or whoever it might be—who had come by train from
Kingswood, Reigate or Epsom, and walked up the dusty
half-mile of road from the little country station of Chipstead, would explain this as they went towards the house to
'take off their things'.

Then I remember the first pings and calling of scores as
tennis began—tennis which was more solemn, more important, than the games played usually on our court. 'A
tennis party' gave the game a sort of sanctity, and we would
be told to sit still and watch while the long-skirted women
and moustached men with white leather belts about their
waists played. And my father, playing, would be lost in the
game, oblivious as only a boy would seem able to be of all
but the ball. His shouts were loud and characteristic. 'I've
got the beast!' of a tricky ball, 'That's luscious!' to a good
stroke of his partner's. Round the court was a high net,
and behind that the peonies and irises and pansies of his
early summer borders. The sun poured down on us and
everyone was happy.

A few of his guests would arrive by motor car, and my
father was considered a shrewd up-to-date and considerate
man because he had put double gates at the top of his garden
with an asphalt square behind them for those brass-lamped
wonders. Their occupants would step down from their high
seats, and the men would remove their goggles while the
women loosened their knotted veils and were led upstairs
by my mother to repair their complexions after the drive.

By lunch-time all who were expected for the meal would
have arrived, for there was none of your telephoning to
warn your hosts that you would be late or unable to come.
An invitation accepted was a bond, and bad manners were
still bad manners, not the pardonable eccentricity of someone. There would be gin and bitters or sherry on a tray
beside the court, where the spectators lay in deck-chairs,
and my father would be persuading some abstemious

woman to drink a second half-glass—for women still expected to be persuaded into drinking alcohol at all. Then, with a gathering up of bags and reticules by the women and an adjustment of silk scarves by the men, the whole gathering would move into the dining-room.

All would be well, and my father at one end of the table and my mother at the other would see that 'the woman' had not 'ruined' the salmon. My father would be wholly occupied in persuading his guests to eat rather more than they would have considered delicate if he had not been there to banter and cajole and force them into it. 'You've got nothing there, Mrs. So-and-So.' 'Now, I'm going to give you a little bit more.' 'Lucy, Mrs. Smith hasn't eaten anything.' Gay, noisy, boyish he appeared as he piled their willing plates.

By half-past two the game would have started again, as guests from nearer at hand who had not been invited to lunch arrived. There were usually twenty to thirty people at my father's tennis parties, and a second court, in a friend's garden nearby, would be used. Under the trees the men would sit and lazily discuss Consuls or cricket, gardening or the next election—the big, absorbing topics of the day. They did not talk of recent books or the Royal Academy, I think, for if it was not a philistine age ours was a philistine circle. They did not often discuss international affairs, for these were still remote and boring to most of them. The women discussed more easily imaginable subjects, for feminine talk in those days had narrower limits. So the nice, plump, happy married women, the nice, slim, mildly flirtatious girls, with piles and coils of hair, high collars and swishing white skirts, sat in deck-chairs with their hems pulled down to their ankles, and discussed sales and clothes and children.

Tea on the lawn, strawberries and cream, my mother being a little flattered by the more dashing of her male guests, coffee ices, and tennis again—I remember how the afternoons went. Then the slow disintegration—'You *must* have a drink before you go'—until finally only the week-end guests were left in the house and the tennis party was over.

My father's guests were mostly people of his own age—in their thirties and forties. They were, I suppose, common-place people, leading conventional uneventful lives and wishing to appear as much like their fellows as possible. Such adjectives as could be found to distinguish them at the time were everyday adjectives—some were 'rich', others 'clever', some 'good', some 'funny'. But all were 'nice'. That was the essential. 'Socialists', people who 'drank', people who were reputed to be 'not quite straight', people who were 'odd' or ill-mannered were not asked to my father's tennis parties.

So from the comfortable villas of Surrey they came, and my father and mother welcomed them. They patronised us children and drew from us odd little children's remarks and generally treated us as though we were a species of intelligent monkey to whom they might presently throw a nut. At the time they had the glamour and greatness of all unfamiliar grown-ups, and in retrospect I feel no antagonism when I remember their complacent pleasant lives, and characters, and faces. They liked my father, recognising in him, perhaps, one of themselves, one who lived as they did, talked, ate, thought, played as they did, but who did all these things with a greater dynamic force than theirs, who seemed impelled by an almost unnatural energy.

I remember many of them and their names. There was Mrs. Castle, a short, determined, middle-aged widow known to be the best woman tennis-player in the region. With her tight mouth and resolute eyes, in fact, she has become for me no more than a tennis-player, as staunchly devoted to the game as Mrs. Battle was to whist. No frivolous conversation round the tea-table for her, no wandering off to look at the garden, but back to the court and the game she loved. Once at a neighbour's house when my father had her as partner he noticed her concealing one of the balls she was supposed to be looking for. 'Don't find it,' she whispered. 'They'll *have* to bring out some new balls in a minute. These are no good.' She was a dedicated woman.

Then there were the Strakers, who lived in a house across the road from Wayside and lent the court for our larger parties. Mr. Straker was a member of the family of London stationers, and the fact that he was 'in trade' could be glossed over by the eminence of his firm. He had a fine baritone voice, and his wife called me over to their house to look at their baby, an experience which made me feel very grown-up.

There was a tall, handsome young architect who also lived in Chipstead whose name was Scott-Willey. His reputation was that of a man used to hunting, for he came from the Shires and wore bold checks. It was at his home that I did one of those unaccountable things of my own volition which caused me to be thought a very odd little boy in those days when children behaved as conventionally as their elders. I knew that the Scott-Willeys kept chickens and that chickens ate worms, and I spent an afternoon collecting earth-worms in the garden, put them in a tin and took them round to present them to Mrs. Scott-Willey, who must have been somewhat baffled by the gift. She realised its good intention, however, and asked me to come to tea next day and present her chickens with the worms. This I did, and remember delicious cakes and Mr. Scott-Willey genially explaining to me that John Peel's coat was not 'so gay', but 'so grey', because the Caldbeck Hunt wore grey coats instead of pink.

Also of Chipstead were Mr. and Mrs. Talbot Smith, who lived in a pretty white house near the village inn. He was—

and is still, I believe—a *Punch* artist, who once delighted the village by caricaturing our local bigwig, Sir Horace Marshall. I remember Mrs. Talbot Smith with devotion, for I once walked across the downs with her and she showed an unpatronising interest in my use of a butterfly-net. But Mr. Talbot Smith's position as an artist produced no eccentricity of appearance, and at our tennis parties he was as welcome as if he had been something as unambiguous as a stockbroker.

They crowd back into my memory, the Barbers already mentioned—tall father, plump, talkative mother and dashing young son, who had just left Christ's Hospital—the doctor who looked after us when we had 'flu, Dr. Tudge, a family called Freeman with a son, Hughie, of my age, and the family of my mother's brother, Edward Taylor, who came over from Woldingham in a Sunbeam motor car driven by a chauffeur called Dench who was a hero of mine because he once drove me at the stupendous speed of thirty miles an hour.

Those were the 'nice' people who came to my father's tennis parties and invited him and my mother to their own, those and more like them in caste and creed. Several of the younger of them were killed in the First World War and their children in the Second, but some at least are living still and may even remember my father's vigorous ebullience as a host.

[2]

When the guests had gone, those friends who had come from a distance and were staying the week-end would go up to dress for dinner. Usually they would be a family called appropriately enough, Smith.

Their friendship dated from my father's days of prosperity at Horley and lasted their lifetimes. Yet for all his name and the fact that he was 'in Mincing Lane' Walter Smith was one of the least commonplace of my father's acquaintances. A man of striking appearance, he stood six foot four, and his face was tanned a fine nut brown, for he had been in the tropics, it was known, and wore a great wide-brimmed Western hat as if to remind one that he was no stay-at-home. He and my father had travelled to Town together every day from Horley. The two were contrasted in appearance—the tall, seasoned, Mincing Lane merchant with the piratical moustache, the brisk, stout, energetic stockjobber. There was an odd, humorous, demonstrative friendship between them such as the top-hatted business-men of those days allowed themselves in periods of relaxation—so that they would be photographed arm-in-arm, and addressed one another, I like to remember, as Big Sweetie and Little Sweetie respectively.

'Mr. Smiff', as he was to me then, was a formidable character among the grown-ups. Most lavish with presents of all who came to our home, he was somewhat frightening to children who scarcely reached his knee. At tennis parties he was an invariable guest, though he rarely played, but sat watching.

'I know what Big Sweetie wants,' my father would say as he sent for the decanter and siphon. Mr. Smith would lie back in his deck-chair with a cheroot and sip the whisky, which he drank in a tumbler filled to the brim with seltzer water, and beam contentedly on everyone.

His wife is less vivid to me, but I remember their son, Jack, and how he brought his fiancée, Gabrielle, down to our home, so that I stared with some interest at two people about to do that inexplicable thing—get married.

The two families had in common an enthusiasm for good food, and the one thing I remember of Mrs. Smith was a little joke she used to make about 'ten minutes' silence' when everyone at table had been served.

F

So after the tennis party, when the Smiths would be at dinner with my father and mother, I would be sent in to say good night. I would be awed by the sight of them sitting round the table in the warm, friendly lamplight—for neither gas nor electricity had reached Chipstead—eating and drinking with unhidden pleasure, while the windows were open to the warm, scented garden and deserted tennis-court, whose net had squeaked down to its release along the ground. I can remember the table set out like one of those elaborate, coloured illustrations in Mrs. Beeton's *Book of Household Management*, and the savoury smell of rich food, and the beautiful gleam of red wine in the lamplight.

Then, when I had been long in bed, I would lie awake listening to my mother playing the piano in the drawing-room under us, playing Beethoven or Mendelssohn or Chopin, the three composers she loved. The music would seem to go across the dark garden as though it had taken form, and I would climb to the window to see the stars in the clear June sky.

A tennis party meant to me as a small boy a day so exciting to the emotions, so wonderful, so eventful that I would be a little too wrought-up and Ninna would come in and say I had overdone it and must get to sleep at once. But this I could not do, for I was going over in my mind again the splendours of the day, as I am doing now, four decades and more after it.

[3]

A different kind of party was that given every year by my father on Boxing Day. This was a family affair, the only guests not our relatives being the Smiths, who, in my mind at least, were as much uncle and aunt as any of the rest of them. It was the one occasion on which Cookes and Taylors met in strength and made a pretty contrast.

We celebrated Christmas Day like any other family with children, stockings hung up and filled, an exchange of presents before breakfast, a dinner (for which all were gathered in the dining-room) of the usual turkey, Christmas pudding, sweets and crackers. It was only on Christmas Day that we children saw the dessert service used, a massive and multifarious affair of Mason's Old Stone china which was brought from the depths of a cupboard to serve nuts and tangerines, grapes and dates and chestnuts which were displayed during the meal as a promise of its climax. I can never see a plate of that pattern now without thinking of ginger in syrup and almonds-and-raisins. There was much playing with new toys, and generally a few tears of fatigue towards the end of the day.

But on Boxing Day was the grown-ups' party, and only those of us who had graduated from nursery to dining-room for meals were present at lunch.

I can remember them arriving—one or other of the hearty Taylor uncles with their jolly wives. They would hang up their thick, lined overcoats which they called 'Ulsters' and greet my father and mother noisily: 'Well, Hubert!' 'Well, Lucy!' Then they threw a 'Well!' to any of us who might be present. Edward Taylor was nearly always there, for he lived a few miles away, Horace (the engineer) more rarely. But sometimes one of the other two was home from abroad—Herbert on leave from the Far East, or Stanley, the youngest, a barrister in Johannesburg, on holiday. They were all good fellows, boisterous and kindly, they were all 'getting on pretty nicely' and meant to enjoy themselves. My father's reputation was to 'do you awfully well' on Boxing Day, and there was always champagne. The Taylor uncles were jocose and appreciative.

Then the Cookes would arrive. 'The Emperor' himself, though he stayed with us several times at Chipstead, never came to these gatherings, but, in the days before Herbert

Cooke had become in my father's invariable phrase 'that scroundel', he was sometimes there, and always the two aunts. Stiff on a straight seat would be my Aunt Xenia, in perpetual mourning for the septuagenarian she had married as a girl. Beaming in another part of the room was my Aunt Eirene, as always, poor dear, a little flushed and over-excited in the presence of men. Her stout, sensible clothes never varied in colour to the end of her life, a severe Puritan grey, and she had gold-rimmed pince-nez.

But my father took these incongruities between the families in his stride. He could make his sisters smile happily and keep his brothers-in-law in check, and find time to look after 'Big Sweetie' and Mrs. Smith and persuade everyone to overeat a little. He would be carving, opening champagne, talking, enjoying his own food and drink, enjoying himself as host. One year my father was called away from his place at the head of the long dining-table, in which the two extra leaves had been inserted, and came back to usher his guests into the hall, for some of the men of the village were mummers that year and, to my huge delight, enacted their *St. George and the Dragon* before our eyes. Later my father would be pressing his guests to stay longer or looking up their trains, the pivot of the occasion, the liveliest and most considerate of them all. He was in his element.

[4]

My father never became a saddened or embittered man and never lost his gusto, but with age his tendency to worry, his fussiness, increased so much that it became something like a mild obsession. It is pleasant for me to think of him as he was at Chipstead before the First World War—carefree, humorous and happy. The prosperity of these days was not quite that of the Kaffir boom, and he now had six children to bring up, but he was making and spending a good deal of money and enjoying both.

All his life an early riser, he would be in the bathroom before I was dressed, and I would watch in fascination while he covered his face with more and more lather, then began to scrape it off with an open razor. While we were at Chipstead there came two changes in my father's life, and it seems remarkable to me that only forty years ago such trivial things should have seemed portentous, not only to me as a child, but to grown-ups as well. He adopted a safety razor instead of a cut-throat, so that when he finished shaving he would let me clean his safety razor and brush for him, and he wore a bowler instead of a silk hat when he went to Town.

After breakfast he would have his walk round the garden and his chat with the gardener then come into the hall.

'Lucy! I'm going now!'

My mother would come and brush his bowler with a little curved brush, and this made a drum-like, hollow sound against the hard felt. I heard it every weekday I spent in my home for thirty years or more, and I can hear it today. On days when it was necessary, my mother would hand him the most neatly rolled umbrella to be seen on Chipstead platform. They would kiss and my father would stride off to the station.

His day in Town was a mysterious thing to me then and not much less today. 'What *is* the Stock Exchange?' I used to ask my father, and from his reply gathered only isolated scraps of information—that it was a place for men who were straight, who dealt in thousands of pounds on their mere word and never went back on it, that it was of great value to 'the country', that my father had to work very hard there for all of us children. My information is still little more than this, but I have gathered some facts about my father's life there at this time—that he was popular, that he showed the same light-heartedness in making money as he did in entertaining and that he gave quick but rather splendid little lunches which were famous. I have spoken to an old man who remembers 'Hubert's lunches' to this day.

He would be back in Chipstead by five or six o'clock, and in summer would go straight into the garden with his hose. He was never happier than when he held this, as he did on summer evenings in all the twenty gardens he made. But in winter we saw little of him after his return, for we were, of course, excluded from 'late dinner'.

As a father he was neither Victorian nor modern, but of his time and class—Edwardian, if you like. He was no tyrant, as his own father had been, but he was more remote than the fathers of today who play and talk and study and live with their children.

Perhaps I have succeeded only in depicting an ordinary little man, perhaps indeed my father was that, and only his son believes in those unusual characteristics of his. For me he remains in memory one of the most interesting and vital of human beings and one of the most endearing. As the young father of six children before the First World War he may have been unremarkable in his achievements, his interests, his conversation, his point of view and his emotions. But he had a quality—or a spark, should I say?—of sheer brilliance, not of intellect, but of character. He knew how to live.

CHAPTER V

Food

[1]

WHEN I come to describe the food we ate it will seem, perhaps, that I am attempting to defend English cooking against that of other nations—France, for instance, or Italy. That would clearly be absurd and is not in the least my intention. But in recalling a household like ours in which my father really cared and knew about food and ate almost nothing but traditional English dishes, I realise that these had, and where they exist still have, real value.

It is fashionable to give a sort of shudder when English cooking is mentioned, and English people who have had a holiday in France and wish to show their cosmopolitanism will tell you that there is not and never has been an English cuisine. But they might remember that in England it is not so much the cooking and certainly not the raw materials that are poor, but public catering. Up and down the country you may search restaurants and hotels one after another for a decent meal, and although here and there by some miracle you may discover one at least edible, you will be forced to admit that the food offered to travellers, visitors, tourists, restaurant-goers of every kind is iniquitous. Every little dirty trick of shady catering is used, even in places of repute, as, for instance, half-boiling a joint of frozen beef, giving it a spell in the oven to produce the semblance of a roast, carving it cold so that the slices may be shaved off more thinly and smothering the result with boiling gravy to deceive the customer with the illusion of a hot meal. Every advantage is taken of the wholesalers' offer to supply the catering trade with huge drums of this or that product, so that scarcely anything one eats has not been preserved in tin and, what little has escaped it, has been frozen, chilled, deep-frozen, dried, desiccated, dehydrated—in some way messed about until none of its pristine savour and nourishment remains. A composition like a stream of custard is used instead of eggs, another is called 'mayonnaise', there are cooking fats of unguessable origins and giant tins of a coloured mess made up of cereals, meat-flavoured, and called veal or beef or ham loaf. Almost all vegetables are tinned ('We can't get enough staff to prepare fresh ones') and there are factory-made mixtures turned out for puddings and cakes. Tinned stews, tongue, ham, jam, butter, milk and fish are all found easier for the cook to handle.

Yet in houses near these hotels and restaurants many English families continue to enjoy English food, cooked as their parents and grandparents cooked it, and at its best it can be very good indeed.

There are several reasons why it has a bad name, apart from the degrading food offered by our caterers. One is that it has been written about by arty and folk-lore-ish persons who have stressed regional dishes of quite uneatable primitiveness and at the drop of a hat will talk of Westmorland wheat-puffs or Essex dunkles. Another is that it is so audaciously simple in method that it must have materials of the finest quality. The English way of cooking green peas, for instance, quite unmixed, unflavoured or uncomplicated, by boiling them in water in which there is nothing but a sprig of mint, is the best method in the world when the peas are young, bright green, full of flavour and gathered an hour before they are cooked. With any lesser, drier or yellower peas it produces something very nasty indeed. In the last twenty years materials for our kind of cookery have been unobtainable, or rare, and the results have been disastrous.

Yet another reason is the disappearance of domestic service. Although in some families cooking has become a hobby, in the majority it is a bore to be got over quickly for the sake of a television programme.

Still, one way or another, the cooking in English homes is better than in public places, and there are still certain dishes, wholly of the British Isles, which bear comparison with anything anywhere. I once won a Concours Gastronomique in France by producing a steak-and-kidney pudding against twenty-eight other national and regional dishes. You will not find these things in restaurants in anything but a degraded form, but you will still find some of them in private homes. I want to write here of the food in my home before the First World War, partly from nostalgia, for I remember it so well, partly as an answer to rather wearisome nonsense about there being no English school of cooking—and no English cooking for that matter—partly as a small incentive to those who do not know some of these truly national dishes to try them, and partly because some of them are in danger of disappearing.

[2]

When we first came to Chipstead I had my meals in the nursery, but soon I was promoted to the dining-room for breakfast and lunch. Breakfast in a family like ours in the last year of King Edward's reign was a large occasion. It was not the breakfast of country house parties, with game pie and grilled salmon and devilled beef at a side table. There would be no more than one cooked dish daily, but that dish was bounteous and excellent.

The English have been called barbarians for their habit

of eating a large meal at the beginning of the day, and with time, I must own, I have almost lost the habit and prefer good coffee and *croissants*. But in childhood I would have thought myself cheated if I had not been able to feel curiosity about 'what's for breakfast'. My father was an early riser and came to the table after an hour in his garden and, barbaric or not, all of us enjoyed those noble meals. Certain English breakfast dishes are unmatched. Indeed I have heard *gourmets* abroad who have found nothing else in England to please them speak soulfully of them. 'Ah, but your English breakfast. That is something!' It certainly was when I was a child.

'Breakfast cereals' were left behind in the nursery. Those paper-like flakes of this or that tasteless husk must have been created to absorb the glutted harvests of America, I feel, and serve no purpose but to distend the bellies of young children or persuade them to swallow a little milk and sugar. Apply some of the cantrips of today to them, talk of vitamins or calories, and you will find poor, earnest mothers spooning them into the mouths of their rebellious children, but what unholy rubbish all this bran and baking amounts to. Before I was seven, thank heaven, I was emancipated from the need to bloat myself with such stuff.

There was frequently fish, and I must have been no more than five when I learned to dissect a kipper, which was still called a kippered herring. But it *was* kippered, its thick, luscious flesh rich from the wood-smoke. It was not the emasculated, oily wretch wrapped in cellophane which is called a kipper today. Or, stronger, a bloater with its delicious hard roe intact. Or fresh herrings which we had plainly grilled at breakfast, though my father used to use a horse-radish sauce. Or smoked haddock—but again it *was* smoked haddock and not a piece of cod or dog-fish or some other tasteless thing coloured yellow and masquerading as haddock, such as one sees on fishmongers' slabs today. Sometimes this is done without deceit and the stuff is labelled 'smoked cod'. But quite often it is a deliberate fake and only by examining the skin of the fish can one tell when purchasing whether or not it is haddock. Once the fish is cooked the difference is instantly perceptible, for true smoked haddock is the result of one of the finest of many curious treatments for fish which the English have invented.

Yet for me the best fish dishes were none of these, but two composite ones—fish-cakes and kedgeree. Of fish-cakes it need only be said that they can be either delectable or odious, and at different times most of us have known both—a blob of bread-crumbed potato faintly flavoured with fish, or the real thing, a mixture of fish, potato, eggs, chopped parsley, carefully formed and proportioned and fried a golden brown.

Kedgeree as we knew it and as it is known today is an example of the way things have, in English kitchens, of growing stereotyped. Originally an Indian dish, *khichri*, of many variations, but with rice and *dal* as its basic ingredients it was first considered in England as a way of preparing any once-cooked fish or meat with hard-boiled eggs and rice. Mrs. Beeton describes various kedgerees made with cold meat, paprika and salmon, while Eliza Acton in her *Modern Cookery* (1845), recommends it for cold turbot, brill, salmon, soles, John Dory and shrimps. By the time I was old enough to eat it, its ingredients were fixed and invariable—smoked haddock, egg and rice. How good it can be, and how simple to make. Cooked rice, drained and not soggy, mixed with broken-up, cooked smoked haddock and chopped-up hard-boiled eggs, with plenty of coarse black pepper and nothing more. It is not a thing to elaborate, and personally I frown even on parsley or nutmeg. Obviously some of the chopped egg is kept to sprinkle over it for the sake of its appearance, and a few sprigs of bright green parsley look well on the dish beside the saffron yellow pile, but otherwise it should be left to recommend itself.

Omelettes were unknown at our breakfast table. Perhaps my parents realised the strange but undeniable fact that whereas any French cook or housewife can make a delicious plain omelette, almost nobody else can. For eggs they were content with the three traditional methods, poaching, boiling, scrambling. My father insisted on cream being added when eggs were being scrambled, but cream in those days cost about 2s. a pint.

It was with bacon that we, like millions of our country-men then and since, usually ate fried eggs. But the bacon would be carefully bought from a supplier whose product was known not to be too salt or too mild, and it was always prime back.

'An economy,' my father would say, for there was no waste with it. There would be streaky or gammon for the kitchen, according to their own preference.

Other accompaniments for bacon were rarer, and there-fore more attractive. Sheep's kidneys, cut with small cross slices so that they were neither too open nor too underdone, were never devilled or prepared in any way which would rob them of their own delightful taste. Mushrooms, in those days before competitive mushroom-growing had produced at forbidding prices huge quantities of tasteless dry fungus, would have been gathered by us from the fields in the early morning or purchased at the back door by the cook from one of the boys of the village. They were simply fried and served with bacon, and I know nothing better.

I cannot resist crying a lament for that masterly creation of the English pork-butcher, the sausage. It has gone, long since, succeeded only by wan parodies, bilious with fat and swollen with old bread, whose proportions have to be controlled by law to ensure that the purchaser secures a little of the gristly flesh of heaven knows what animal. The sausage of my childhood was not a repository for the machine-minced skin and offal of a pork-butcher's chopping block; it was made in competition with other sausage-makers and it sold on its own reputation. 'Brown's sausages are very good.' 'I like sausages from the Stores.' Each his preference, but no maker could have survived on the rancid miscellany packed into skins today. Pork neither too fat nor too lean our sausages had, a little veal perhaps, lest they were too rich, breadcrumbs, but not too many, and flavourings known only to their makers, flavourings with which they sought to characterise their own product—nutmeg, lemon-rind, cinnamon perhaps, certainly sage leaves and a few other herbs, none of them too potent for the delicate whole.

They will never come again and not all the advertising of the factory-owners, who now turn out sausages of a kind by the million, will ever convince my generation that they will. With a flick of mustard and a piece of bread fried in the unadulterated fat which had run from them, they made a food for gods and those lucky mortals born long enough ago to have known them.

Breakfasts were not always hot, for once or twice a year my father would buy a York ham, or a Stock Exchange acquaintance ('I made a lot of money for that man') would send him a ham as a gift. Or there would be a tongue cooked and pressed under my mother's supervision, not pulled out of a tin smothered in gelatine and tasting of nothing at all. Or a Bath chap, that excellent little pig's cheek which could be bought whole, ready cured and may occasionally be found today. Or brawn, which my mother also made herself in a big, round press, a brawn large enough to last most families too long, but for our hungry household of eleven not too large to keep its interest to the end. Or cold

pickled pork or cold bacon, on which each of us opened a
boiled egg.

When that was eaten, there would be toast and home-
made marmalade or for my father his favourite delicacy,
smoked cod's roe. Sometimes there was potted meat made
from the last of the family joint by mincing the meat,
adding salt, pepper, a little ground cloves and nutmeg and
a touch of anchovy essence, then sealing the whole in a jar
under melted butter. Two familiar white jars stood also
on our breakfast table, one of anchovy paste made by the
old and honourable firm of Burgess, a paste which has not
degenerated even today, the other *Patum Peperium*, 'the
Gentleman's Relish', for the sake of which, last week, I
made the crossing from Tangier, where my home is, to
Gibraltar, in which it can be obtained.

Splendid, leisurely breakfasts with natural but not
noisy chatter, with time for my father to eat in peace before
his walk to the station and for us to eat with our heads full
of plans for the day. The dining-room at Wayside overlooked the tennis court and the laurel hedge beyond it, so
that as I sat at breakfast in the corner seat beside my father
I could munch and think and look out to the garden, a very
happy little boy.

[3]

Other meals in my home were as simple. There was
occasionally soup, but more often a single dish of either fish
or meat and always a number of vegetables. These would
be followed by what my parents called a 'sweet' and sometimes there was cheese. But anything like a succession of
courses would have been unthinkable—'too much washing-
up for the servants'.

Soups at home were not made strictly to recipe any more
than they are in the ordinary homes of France. With a

kitchen range lighted before seven in the morning and kept
going all day, it was easy to have a stock-pot in which
bones, for instance, could have the five or six hours necessary to extract their nourishment. Our soups were character-
ised chiefly by their vegetable contents, which changed
with the season—celery, tomatoes, peas or Jerusalem
artichokes. Those dominated by meat were straightforward
—oxtail, kidney, rabbit, hare, chicken. In vegetable soups,
I remember, a good deal of barley was used, and for
all cream soups there would be little croutons of fried
bread.

In fact, the soups we had on occasion came as near to the
classic form as soup usually does. Anywhere but in one of
the eleven restaurants of France accredited by the com-
pilers of the *Michelin Guide* with three roses, the terminology
of soups is used loosely, so that such a name as *Brunoise*
means very little to one ordering a meal. When in my home
the last of a chicken was used to make a clear soup it was
not called *consommé de volaille* and, although the stock-pot and
vegetable garden gave us what could perfectly well have
borne the titles *Jardinière, Julienne* or *Printanière*, to us they
were simply soup.

When I go on to claim that the sternest simplicity was
used also in the treatment of fish and swear that because of
the high quality of the fish my father chose and brought
home it was effective, I shall be accused of carrying an
argument too far. But it is not so. What English cooking
had—and where it survives still has—is daring. It dismisses
complicated flavours and the use of too many ingredients
and concentrates on the principal one. It is less sophisticated
and intricate than any other European system, not because
the English have in the past been ignorant or lazy cooks,
but because the superb quality of English meat, fish and
vegetables enable it to be. Truly English sauces, for instance
can be numbered on the fingers of two—perhaps one—

hands and stuffings only appear when they are essential and not whenever they are pleasant.

So, although my father knew a great deal about food, the fish we ate was prepared without unnecessary garnishes or sauces. Plaice and sole we always had *à la Meunière*, with only a piece of lemon to adorn them. Turbot and salmon were poached, and the salmon served with melted butter and sliced cucumber, the turbot with melted butter or Hollandaise sauce. It would have seemed sacrilege to my father to eat lobster in any way but cold, with a mayonnaise which my mother made herself of a deep yellow richness which I have not seen bettered since.

Other invariably used methods were 'sousing' for mackerel, frying in deep fat for whitebait, and baking for whiting—this last a dish I detested and have never liked since. But more variety had to be found for that dull brute the cod, which in any case was apt to appear, if at all, at lunch on weekdays when my father was in London. It had been in salt water overnight, an essential measure, and it would come to the table in steaks or poached with anchovy sauce or plenty of parsley butter. Its roe was pounded into a delicious fish-paste which lasted several days.

Scallops were a favourite of my father's, and I am grateful for it. Prime both in taste and consistency, they are less expensive than other shellfish and more satisfying. We used to have them cooked in several ways, not because they needed variation, but because they were so delectable in each that my father found it hard to make up his mind. 'I think we'll have those scallops stewed,' he would suggest, but might change it to 'in their shells'.

One of my mother's gifts was for dressing a crab. 'Are you going to do it yourself?' my father would ask anxiously when he had brought down from London the largest crab he could find. Then my mother would dress it, patiently gathering all the fragments to return to the shell, mixed with a little vinegar, olive oil, salt and black cayenne pepper. She would sprinkle it with chopped-up hard-boiled egg and find some garnish for its dish before it came to table. Again—completely simple and completely effective. Madame Prunier, in her splendid *Fish Cookery Book*, gives seven ways of presenting a crab, and her garnishes include lobster sauce and truffles. Yet I believe she would agree that nothing suits this elaborately flavoured shell-fish better than plain dressing.

Meat in my home was treated with the same confidence. My father bought only English or Scotch beef, and wanted it roast simply and in no way messed about. Canterbury lamb, which nowadays seems to be called New Zealand lamb, he maintained was excellent, but preferred English. These and joints of pork and veal were always roast and served with the traditional accompaniments: with beef a sauce made from horse-radish straight from the garden, with mutton mint sauce or red-currant jelly, with veal sage and onion and with pork a sharp apple sauce. My heart sinks a little when I remember what are too often served in place of these today—mass-manufactured horse-radish sauce, mint sauce made from dried mint and vinegar, *ersatz* red-currant jelly, desiccated sage shaken out of a packet on to bread pulp and shredded onion, even tinned apple *compôte*.

No less in the convention of the time and no less excellent were those other married couples of the kitchen—roast beef and Yorkshire pudding, boiled silverside and dumplings, calf's head and parsley sauce, boiled pork and pease pudding boiled mutton and caper sauce, liver and bacon, tripe and onions. They all sound rather heavy and Victorian, like an early edition of *Mrs. Beeton*, and one can imagine them being served in stuffy dining-rooms in Dickens's day. But most of them go back farther than that, to the eighteenth century and farther, and some of them, at their best, are grand.

G

Clearly, if you parboil your beef to make more of it and produce a Yorkshire pudding that looks and tastes like rubber, if your dumplings are leaden and your calf's head insipid for lack of flavouring, if your pease pudding is dry and solid and your boiled mutton tough and tired, your liver leathery and your tripe tasteless—obviously then nothing can be expected of these combinations but nausea. But a good cook with the right materials can make of almost every one of them a splendid dish.

It was the same story with parts of the animal other than sirloin or ribs of beef, leg or shoulder or saddle of mutton, loin of pork or veal, which usually made our joints. Mutton chops and steak were both grilled, and the latter served with very finely shredded onion rings which had been fried in deep fat to give them a feathery crispness, and often with grilled tomatoes. With both there were always chipped potatoes, which were not shaved off as game chips or the salted, papery flakes sold in packets now, but cut in long, flat-sided sticks.

Sweetbreads appeared in a number of guises, for they were a favourite with my father, fried, braised, stewed, with only vegetables and herbs used in the cooking and no elaborate sauce. Sheep's hearts had a stuffing of sage and onion, grated lemon peel and spices. Ox-tail appeared in a rich gravy—one of the few meat dishes for which wine was used in our kitchen.

Two other dishes we had, which can be excellent or can be debased to a feeble mockery of food, were steak-and-kidney pudding and Irish stew. I have elsewhere written with enthusiasm, if not ecstacy, of that magnificent and wholly English dish, the steak-and-kidney pudding, in which the flavour is imprisoned by the suet pastry for the five hours during which it is steamed, giving to the resulting gravy and meat a richness of taste and consistency obtainable in no other way known to me. I was shocked the other day when a man of some discrimination and knowledge in food said that he preferred a steak-and-kidney pie, that more pretentious but infinitely less flavoursome cousin of the pudding. How can it achieve distinction except as a stew which has been covered with crisp or flaky pastry? The whole point of the pudding is the long hours in which the meat slowly softens and blends with the herbs and spices, which must be used lightly, so strongly does everything sealed inside the thick blanket of white suet pastry keep its flavour.

An Irish stew is more difficult to produce in perfection, for the ingredients allowable by tradition are so few that success depends wholly on the cook's gift for timing and flavouring and the quality of the materials. Its basis, of course, as even today any English cook knows, is mutton (neck or cutlets or preferably both) stewed with potatoes. But it is uninteresting if onions, carrots, chopped herbs and just the right quantity of salt and pepper are not added, and it may have a leek or two, a head of celery, even mushrooms without wholly losing its good peasant character. Ours had dumplings dropped in after it had simmered for a while.

[4]

We ate roast chicken with bread sauce—a custom which has brought more derision than any other on the heads of English cooks. In another book I wrote of it: 'Foreigners have asked plaintively why we serve this tasteless pap with roast chicken or pheasant, but that is chiefly because bread sauce is often badly made. Carefully done, the bread rubbed through a sieve to ensure fineness, a thin white stock used, a grating each of onion and nutmeg, a clove, some butter and enough of salt and pepper, and you have something that may justly be called a relish, while a little cream will give it distinction.' But it was a more serious fault in my home that we never had chicken in any other way but roast with bread sauce, or, as invalid food, boiled with white sauce. This, I think was not because other ways were unknown—after all, *Mrs. Beeton* was in the house and could provide more than seventy—but because my father liked it best. At least it was never *rechauffé*, and never appeared in fragments. Plainly roast also were duck, goose and turkey, though stuffing and sauces for the last two were various and good.

Game was rarer and limited to roast pheasant and patridge. I remember no venison, grouse or quail, for instance, and only once or twice young pigeons *en casserole*.

But a crowning glory of that long mahogany table in our dining-room at Chipstead was one of our sovereign national dishes—jugged hare. This I maintain is the finest way of cooking hare in the world, and nothing that France or Hungary can produce compares with it, though these are the other two countries in which the hare is appreciated most and cooked best.

It brought out all the skill and flair in my home, for whatever cook we happened to have it was my mother who gave precise instructions. If it is to be successfully jugged, a hare must be kept hung by its hind legs and a receptacle tied under its head to keep the blood. This was done and a little vinegar and water put in to prevent the blood from coagulating.

The hare was skinned and drawn in my mother's presence and the liver and heart retained. Then it was cut up and put into a marinade of wine, bay-leaves, thyme, cloves, sliced onion, chopped garlic, vinegar and water and left for a night, or longer if it was an old hare. The pieces were browned in a frying pan and cooked in a casserole in stock and red wine with the chopped heart and liver, browned onions, shallots, chopped bacon, cloves, lemon-juice, cinnamon and bay-leaves. When it was about to be served, a couple of glasses of port went in, and the dish was served with forcemeat balls and red-currant jelly. It was magnificent.

[5]

Our vegetables were always straight from the garden. Gardeners are notoriously difficult to keep out of the kitchen garden; countrymen themselves, they understand and care for vegetables more than rare plants. My father's gardener at Chipstead was like that. He produced vegetables of superlative quality in great abundance, and these came to the table in almost pristine state, boiling in water being all the preparation given to most of them. On the whole, I think they justified this.

A few of them were allowed a Bechamel sauce, notably Jerusalem artichokes, broad beans, vegetable marrow, salsify, cauliflower and leeks. A few of them really needed a clever sauce or more cunning preparation—French beans, for instance, cabbage and spinach. But young peas, Brussels sprouts, tender scarlet runner beans, broccoli, new potatoes—how could these have been improved? A little butter was all they had or needed.

In winter potatoes were always roasted with the joint, and this gave my parents a sort of testing-ground for any cook they employed. If she could send them in crisp and brown with a crust a quarter of an inch thick and the interior floury and dry she was a treasure. If they came in moist and desolate-looking she was no good. My father would look at these pale potatoes disgustedly.

'Waxy brutes,' he would say.

I think he was right to be a little exigent about this. It is one of the best ways of cooking any but new potatoes, but it requires a little trouble and frequent basting.

Root vegetables were by no means treated contemptuously, as one finds them so aften treated nowadays. Parsnips of pale saffron colour, creamed turnip, that delicious thing salsify, the vegetable oyster as it is rightly called, Jerusalem artichokes with their own nutty flavour—all these I remember well. Carrots were used only in stews and soups, I think, but braised onions and braised celery were popular.

Celery was and for most of us will always be one of our compensations for the English winter. It grows better in the British Isles than anywhere, and to the English belongs the credit of discovering that God created it to be eaten with cheese. The French have not yet realised this simple truth and use it only in *hors d'œuvres* and as a vegetable braised. The ambrosial combination of a scoop of fine ripe Stilton with crisp sticks of celery has not yet occurred to them.

If it is the most attractive vegetable of winter, then asparagus is its summer counterpart. But not the inch-thick, flabby, candle-white muck out of tins which appears in most restaurants. It should be purple-tipped, dark green asparagus of medium thickness just cut in the garden. It can only be dipped in melted butter and eaten with the fingers as we were taught to eat it as children after we had firmly tucked our table napkins into our collars for the purpose. (We called them serviettes, by the way, and it still seems to me a more correct and less pretentious name than any other.)

My father took special care of the things he grew for summer salads. Lettuces, both cos and cabbage, were cut before the sun was on them and came into the house crisp and cool. Tomatoes from the greenhouse or the open ground were not picked until they were ripe, never ripened in the dark. I can hear my father now calling me over to help him lift the glazed top of the frame in which he grew cucumbers of great length and beauty. Mustard and cress from a dark place in the greenhouse had long white stems. Oval radishes and thick spring onions were timed to appear throughout the salad season. But the most important thing for my father was chive.

'It's the making of a salad,' he used to say as he cut a handful with a pair of scissors for my mother to snip over the other things when she had mixed them.

She always made the salads herself and they contained the things I have mentioned and nothing else. None of those repulsive American miscellanies was ever put before us, salads in which fruit and vegetables and heaven knows what nuts and flower petals or, for all I know, jam and cheese have been mixed. In a modern cookery book I have seen advocated apples, bananas, walnuts, grated cheese, honey and sour cream as elements to harmonise with lettuce, cucumber and water-cress. Well, if you like that sort of thing I suppose you should be free to eat it, but why call it salad, which the *Concise Oxford Dictionary* defines as 'a cold dish of uncooked usually sliced vegetables, such as lettuce or endive seasoned with oil, vinegar, etc.'

My mother kept within that definition, adding only a hard-boiled egg cut in thin slices as a garnish. She would mix the whole in a huge glass dish which with a pair of oddly shaped 'salad-servers' had been one of the less useless of her wedding-presents. And she would mix the salad-dressing herself, using eggs and oil, vinegar, mustard, salt, pepper and cream.

'Eat plenty of green stuff, my boy,' said my father. 'It's so good for you.'

Only when I came to live in warm climates did I realise the good fortune of the English and French, whose climate and soil give them the finest vegetables in the world. In India, for instance, one sees in the vegetable bazaar the most enticing display, great, deep-coloured tomatoes, clean-looking new potatoes, pale, swollen lettuces, bright, crisp cucumbers—yet when one eats them, remembering their fellows in our harsher climate, one finds them almost tasteless. Around the Mediterranean the same thing is noticeable, and even South Africa and Argentina, which produce glorious fruit and vegetables, cannot infuse into them that delicate yet persistent flavour which is in English green peas and new potatoes. I am glad to have been brought up on them.

[6]

To us as children I need hardly say it was 'the sweet', 'the pudding' or 'the dessert' that was of most interest. This too has been counted a gastronomical sin against the English, that we excel in an art which in most civilised countries is considered more the confectioner's than the cook's. Moreover, I admit that for most of my adult life I rebelled against such lack of proportion in planning a meal and never thought of anything but cheese or fruit as its tailpiece. But now at fifty odd I find myself returning to at least a mild interest in such things and certainly remembering kindly the puddings of my childhood.

This is no place to list or describe them, for they at least are in no danger of disappearing even if, too often, they are made from packets of ready-mixed ingredients. However 'plain' a cook might be, however lacking in finesse in other things, at least she was adept at these, and sent them to the table under the rather grand names which Mrs. Beeton gave them: Queen of Puddings, Apple Charlotte, Almond Castles, Cabinet Pudding, Baroness Pudding, Charlotte Russe, Kaiser Pudding, Empress Pudding, Windsor Pudding and so on—names which recall to me the inverted pudding-basin shapes which appeared under their sauces and the taste of sultanas, raisins, almonds, ginger, lemon and the rest which went into them. There were more plebeian names, Apple Dumplings, Batter Pudding, Semolina, Betsy, Bread-and-Butter, Roly-poly, Cottage, Hasty and Omnibus puddings, but I cannot remember that they were any less highly thought of, at least by me.

There were also many stewed fruits—never called *compôtes*—with jellies made in curiously shaped moulds, detestable blancmange and delicious nutmeg-strewn junket.

Only two things seem to me worth recalling from this sweet catalogue, a sherry trifle and a fruit salad. In the book I wrote on sherry I eulogised the former: 'It was made with sponge cake baked in the house. This sponge cake was made with eggs—and I mean eggs which had recently been laid by a hen, not some thick, yellow liquid poured from a tin in the modern machine bakery. The jam that was between the layers of sponge-cake was also home-made, not a compound of chemicated pulps and saccharine, coloured and sprinkled with manufactured pips. These were covered with cream which, again, was not a sweet, white paste, but the result of hard work with an egg-whisk in a bowl of cream from the local dairy, unpasteurised, unhygienic perhaps, but quite delicious. The whole was stuck with split almonds to give it a hedgehog appearance, somebody troubling to skin and split the almonds with a knife. But before the cream was added, the sherry was poured over, and it was a sherry which the cook could, and probably did, drink.'

A good fruit salad is no chancy collection of fruits haphazardly jumbled. It would take my mother an hour or two on the day before we were to have one of these to assemble and prepare it. It was made entirely from summer fruits from the garden, except for one pleasantly conflicting ingredient, thick slices of banana. Strawberries, raspberries, red, white and black currants, stoned cherries, grapes, peaches, apricots, nothing pulpy and nothing that needed cooking. These were mixed in a large earthenware bowl, smothered with sugar and left for the night so that juice formed itself. They were eaten next day with cream. Now go out and buy yourself a tin of fruit salad of yellow

California peaches, slices of pineapple and pear and a couple of Maraschino cherries.

Cheese appeared with guests, for the most part, and came to the table in another odd utensil which had been a wedding present, a silver basket in three divisions, one each for cheese, butter and biscuits. A ripe Camembert, Pommel, Gorgonzola and Gruyère were the only foreign cheeses we ever had, for my father swore by English cheese and would 'order from the Stores' double Gloucester or Cheddar loaf, and at Christmastime always an entire Stilton.

Coffee after a meal was also reserved for days on which there were guests, and we would have been 'allowed to get down' before it was served.

[7]

But there was another meal for us children—tea. Not for some years yet did I have dinner with my parents, and in the meantime ate at half-past four in the nursery a meal of bread and butter, jam and cake.

The jam was always home-made. I remember the days in summer and autumn when the big copper preserving pan appeared and jam was made by my mother and Ninna. They both enjoyed this and made only a feeble pretence about the cook having enough to do already. They would sit on the lawn preparing the fruit, removing stalks or stones, then leave it under sugar for the required time and boil it. I remember the anxious moments when some was put on a plate to see if it would 'set'. I remember the jam itself in the jam cupboard upstairs to which I would be taken when I was going back to school to choose two pots of whichever kind I liked. I do not suppose it was better than jam made in countless English homes then and today, but it was incomparably better than the manufactured jams even of those days before the factory-owners had learnt half the tricks of mass production they know today. I simply cannot understand how anyone, in whose household it is eaten, accepts as jam the ready-made mixture of vegetable pulp and pectin, tartaric acid, starch, glucose and beet sugar, coloured by aniline dyes and called wistfully after some fruit or other, when it is possible to make real jam at home. I suppose it is because there is 'no time'. There was time in Edward VII's reign, however, and no mass-manufactured jam, marmalade or jelly was given to us.

Cakes, too, were made at home, and there was usually a solid and fruity monster on the nursery table.

Sometimes I would be called by my mother to hand round cakes and sandwiches to her guests at an afternoon tea-party, for in those days ladies in a place like Chipstead found pleasure in dressing carefully, walking to the house of their hostess, sitting in the drawing-room or in summer on the lawn, balancing pretty china tea-cups, chatting vigorously for an hour or two while the best that could be offered them in bread and butter, sandwiches and cakes, was handed round on three-tiered cake-stands. Next week it would be for one of them to be hostess and while they exchanged kindly gossip they noted the new chair-covers and the fillings of sandwiches.

A ladies' tea-party must sound dull to the present inhabitants of those same houses at Chipstead, who certainly cannot spare the time for such feeble diversions. Even if they have not got jobs, they have a thousand things to do and a car to do them in. Besides, they are not acquainted with people merely because they happen to live in the same village, and no one has paid an 'afternoon call' for twenty years or more. Then they have no servants in shining white caps and aprons to open the door and bring in the silver tray, and if they are going to entertain at all would rather ask people for a drink.

When I think of my mother's 'at homes' it seems truly that they must have happened centuries ago in a place more resembling Cranford than our world. Yet there are people still living in Chipstead who came to them, and to me they are more vivid than last night's cocktail party.

What delicious things I used to carry round. Bread and butter cleverly cut and spread to be rolled into little tubular shapes, brown and white. Cucumber sandwiches lightly peppered, anchovy paste or smoked cod's roe sandwiches, mustard-and-cress sandwiches, all of them cut that afternoon by a cook who expected the 'extra work' of a tea-party from time to time. In winter hot things appeared from under silver lids, crumpets, toast, muffins, tea-cakes. And winter and summer there were 'fancy cakes', which were required to be delicate and light in appearance because the convention was that none of the ladies was hungry.

They were baked in things called patty-pans, and I do not suppose that many young housewives today would know what the word means. The batter, made with half a dozen eggs, no doubt, would be mixed and variously flavoured, some with almond, some lemon, some coconut, then dabbed into the six convex circles in each tin and baked. Sometimes they were still warm from the oven when my mother's guests arrived, but in that case they were forbidden to me as 'indigestible'.

The ladies would nibble them appreciatively, but there would always be plenty of them for nursery tea later. There would always be plenty of everything in Surrey before the First World War—plenty to eat and drink, plenty to do and above all plenty of time. For the prosperous middle classes it was an age of plenty.

CHAPTER VI

The Village

[1]

CHIPSTEAD THEN was a village, not a dormitory district under the protection of the Green Belt Scheme. It had a life of its own and its inhabitants, though they kept in their social categories, were held together by ties, obligations and even a little loyalty.

Much of this life was centered on the church and the village hall, some on the White Hart. The community was further bound together by the annual fête and flower-show, by the fact that the men walked to the same station and travelled together every day and the women, as we have seen, met at one another's houses.

Socially there were three strata—'gentle-people', 'common people' and 'village people'. The 'gentle-people' included all the professional families and some superior 'trade' and created the social life of the village. The 'common people' were the near misses, the pretentious and the vulgar, people who might live in houses like those of the 'gentle-people' and be even more prosperous than they, yet were not acceptable in their circles. The 'village people' belonged to the working class, lived in cottages and frequently—this will startle the younger generations—frequently touched their caps to the 'gentle people' they knew. I have even seen a curtsy made.

There were nice points of etiquette. Ninna, if this had been today, would have been more or less articulately of the left wing. I remember that my parents thought it droll that she should teach me to use the word 'Mr.' for 'village people', speaking of 'Mr.' Peckham and 'Mr.' Barnard as though these, farm foreman and mechanic respectively, were 'gentle-people'. Mr. Barnard, as a matter of fact, was a go-ahead man and started a small shop in the village. My father liked him, I think, but found him a 'good-as-you-are kind of fellow'. There was no squire, the occupant of the largest house being Sir Horace Marshall, who as a whole-sale newsagent was quite unacceptable among the 'gentle-people'.

The 'village people' were poor by any standards and however it may be argued that you could buy so much more for a shilling. My father's gardener earned 25s. a week and was considered in the village to occupy an enviously well-paid position. Few families could afford more than candle-light in the evening, and water had to be fetched from the village pump. There were boot clubs, clothing clubs, coal clubs by which the more prudent sought to ensure their winter supply. There was, it is true, a great deal of private and local charity for the deserving, but it was charity with some, if not all, the odious features of charity as Dickens described them. No. The working people may have been happier in those days, but they were certainly not better off.

However, most of the men found the means to do two things—take a pint or two at the White Hart on Saturday night and produce their families sufficiently well-dressed on Sunday morning to attend the parish church. The 'Sunday suit', a rigid affair in black or dark blue which lasted for years, has not completely disappeared from rural England, but in those days it was invariably a feature of the Sabbath.

[2]

It may well be realised, then, that it was an event of major importance to the village when 'old Mr. Harvey' the Rector, decided to retire and his place was taken by a certain Canon Stone. People who 'didn't go to church' were rare in those days and not well thought-of, whatever their status, so that few were wholly unaffected by the change. Church—the sermon, the singing of hymns in chorus, the observation of one another—was all that many of them had as an occasion, not only for voicing religious and other sentiments, but for entertainment as well. Radio was still (what it could have remained, so far as I am concerned) a means of communication between ships at sea. The nearest cinema was at Purley, a train journey away; there was perhaps one village concert a year and no lending library. So the village church with its organ and community singing was a centre for more than worship.

Canon Stone was what was called an enlightened or progressive churchman, though more strictly 'low church' than his predecessor. I remember him as a tall, distinguished looking man with a gift of humour, one of the few grown-ups of my childhood whose teasing or leg-pulling I did not, consciously or otherwise, resent. He was reputedly a fine preacher and though I was a child when I heard him, there remains to me now the impression of an ardent, eloquent man in the pulpit. Besides, one phrase he used suggests a broad and probably intelligent outlook.

'That grand old materialist, Napoleon Buonaparte . . .' I remember him saying, though the rest of the sentence is lost.

At all events my father, who never went to church before or after the days of Canon Stone, took to coming with us on Sunday mornings, and praised the new Rector as a 'very fine chap'.

Under Canon Stone's régime a new discipline was introduced among the churchgoers of Chipstead. His wife and daughters were strict assistant shepherds and if one of the flock had strayed would notice it.

'Is your husband not well today?' they would sternly ask my mother as we left the church on a Sunday when his garden had been too strong a counter-attraction for my father, a question put even more bluntly to 'village people', who were asked why someone was not in church.

[3]

Not every inhabitant of the village, however, was a member of Canon Stone's congregation or could be dropped into one of the three social categories. One remarkable exception was Dr. Freshfield, who lived in a house on the road to Reigate and was, my father told me, a Freeman of the City of London.

I saw him only once and perhaps the years have given a false magic to the occasion, though I do not want to think so. It was a summer evening and there was a beautiful but disturbing sunset. I do not know why I was with my father and mother, nor can I guess what took them to Dr. Freshfield's house. But we arrived there at about five o'clock and found him alone.

He was a small man, grey-haired with a short beard and merry grey eyes. He was immensely loquacious—indeed, it seems as I look back to that evening that he never for a moment stopped talking. Everything about him and his house seemed to me exotic and interesting.

He had been, I believe, a great traveller in the East and spoke and wrote a number of Oriental languages, including Arabic. I remember him saying that he had been accepted somewhere by some people as a Mohammedan.

But it was the things around him which awed and attracted me, the things he showed us and the things at which I could stare. There were great manuscript Arabic books exquisitely illuminated, there were strange swords and knives with jewelled handles, there was jade, ivory, silver and gold, there were embroidered curtains and gorgeous carpets.

But most wonderful were the flowers. We went into a greenhouse which adjoined the house and he showed my father plants he had brought with him from abroad and gave my mother a curious tubular wax flower such as I have never seen since. All his flowers were strange to me and to my father, I think, and he talked endlessly about them.

It is the sense of wonder I felt which returns to me now across the years. The house was Aladdin's cave, not of the pantomime, but of the immortal story itself. Dr. Freshfield, narrating, exhibiting, explaining, belonged to no familiar world, but was a being apart, touched by the mysteries and enchantments of the East as I knew them from fairy stories. I did not speak and I cannot remember that my parents did more than make a few brief, encouraging responses to that monologue. It was as though we were under a spell.

Then we went into the garden and Dr. Freshfield showed us an orange tree, explaining in vigorous phrases that there had once been two, but when his wife was ill the other sickened and when she died it died with her.

'If I see this tree at all off colour, I tell the gardener to give it every care he can,' added Dr. Freshfield with a comically rueful look as he led us back to the house.

I cannot remember why, but we went upstairs and our host opened a cupboard and pulled out a beautiful little rug which he almost threw at my mother.

'I would like you to have it,' he said. 'It's a prayer mat from . . . ' I have forgotten its origin and I am ashamed to ask an expert, as I could now, because the little rug is beside

H

me. It is, I have been told, of considerable value, so finely woven that those who know carpets wonder at the number of stitches to the square inch. It remained with my parents through all the vicissitudes which followed them, through all their moves and refurnishings, and it has remained with me through mine.

With it most vivaciously has lived the memory of the man who gave it and his marvellous house. It is forty-seven years since I saw him on that single occasion and I have never wished to find out more about him, how he came to possess his treasury of materials and knowledge or why he was a Freeman of the City of London. But I know now that once for an hour he took me out of the smug world which was all I knew and opened magic casements. Thereafter there was such a place as 'the East', not only in books (after all anything could be in books), but in actual fact. Dr. Freshfield had been there.

[4]

There were two other old gentlemen in Chipstead who in my memory at least resembled Dr. Freshfield in appearance, though perhaps this is only because all three wore beards. One was Mr. Cheeseman, who lived in a square white house hidden behind lodge gates and, like my father, went to the Stock Exchange each day. He was no more than a silk hat, a frock coat and a white beard to me and I dare say I should have forgotten his existence if he had not presented us with half a dozen white fantail pigeons which were the first pets I was allowed to possess.

A pigeon-house was constructed for them in which were nesting boxes, and they soon increased. I can remember the look of the young swollen bodies sprouting their first quills, but better I can remember the smell of them and of all the pigeons, a sweet-and-sour smell which has never been in my nostrils since.

For me they were 'carrier pigeons', and I would take one in a basket to a far hillside and, after tying a message to his leg, release him. The messages were not in code, but were secret and sometimes of fearful moment—'Surrounded by savages. Please come to the rescue', or 'Have found the treasure. Will mark spot'. It was thrilling to reach home half an hour later to find that the message had been safely delivered.

The other old gentleman demonstrated that the lunacy laws, like others, were interpreted with more wisdom and charity at that time, for today he would certainly not be allowed to remain at large. Yet what harm was there in old Mr. Tucker, who lived in his own house and never left it without a male attendant? I met him once when I was wandering alone on a hillside near the village and was quite unafraid when he spoke to me. 'I've half a mind to give you sixpence to buy a new hat with,' he said while his attendant smiled kindly.

Less eccentric but by reputation no less mean was the widow who owned a little farm adjoining Wayside, a Mrs. Flint. She certainly looked rather severe and tight-lipped, a neat, business-like old lady to whom I would be sent to purchase eggs at 9d. a dozen. I liked going to her house because it lay across a field of lazy cows and in its name at least had the attraction of being a farm. Her reputation for avarice was based on the fact that, instead of giving to her gardener prizes won by her in the annual flower show, the half-sovereign for best display of vegetables and so on, she divided the prize with him. She and her gardener have been dead these thirty years or more and her sin does not seem so serious at this distance, but in Chipstead at that time it was doing something which no one else did and was spoken of with abhorrence.

[5]

Of my contemporaries, the children to whose homes I would be asked to tea-parties, I have no very clear or happy recollections.

There was a large family of hearty children called Lambert who seem in retrospect—unjustly, no doubt—to have been noisy and oafish. There was Hughie Freeman, a boy with an exciting pedal motor car. He died shortly afterwards and the unfamiliar and unpleasant idea of death erased the earlier recollections.

There was also Esmée Bull. She was a child of my own age with whom I had a forced and difficult acquaintance which was occasioned by Ninna's intimacy with her nurse.

'Now you two children walk on it front,' we would be told while Ninna and her friend talked long and in low tones.

Esmée Bull no doubt grew into a handsome and amiable woman, but seemed to me the most dislikable of all little girls, who were in any case not the companions one sought at seven years old. She wore glasses and told me that she had to do exercises with her eyes each day, 'trying to make a bird hop into a cage', to correct a strabismus. I resented having to walk with a little girl, and when I had been at a preparatory school for a term and had learnt to throw the immemorial abuse of small boys—'silly ass', 'frightful fool', and so on—I used one of the commonest terms among members of the lowest form and called Esmée Bull a guttersnipe.

This produced reactions which still seem to me rather exaggerated. Esmée Bull at once turned round and told her nurse, and Ninna expressed her grief and shock by taking me straight home to bed. My parents were informed of my crime and tried to bring home to me the heinousness of it.

'How dare you use such a word to a little girl? I don't know how you came to know such a word.'

'No gentleman would ever speak to a little girl like that.'

I was not articulate enough to defend myself by saying what was perfectly true, that I was simply repeating a recognised piece of school repartee. I was not applying the word to Esméee Bull. I did not know at all what it meant. I was told that I had been guilty of nothing so grave since at the age of three I threw my grandmother's jewellery out of the window. But once again it was a case of assessing the gravity of a child's offence by its consequence to grown-ups. In this case my parents, who for some reason had not called on the Bulls when they came to Chipstead, now felt they must go and apologise to them for my shocking behaviour.

[6]

My afternoon walks with Ninna continued during school holidays long after I had been sent as a boarder to a preparatory school—in fact, till I was eight or nine years old. The way I liked most was up a steep slope of the downs to a path along the crest of the hill. Beside this path for several hundred yards the ponticum rhododendrons made a great pile of colour and I have loved all rhododendrons ever since.

But it was here that we came on a horror, a wild squeaking in a thicket, a rabbit with its neck in a wire noose, with distended eyes and helpless, jerky movements. I had never seen a rabbit-snare before; I did not know how to release the slip-knot and did not find the way to do it for several agonising moments. Even afterwards, when I had seen the little creature scuttle away, I did not realise at first that it had been deliberately snared, that this cruelty was human work. I thought it had got caught in a piece of wire.

It would be pleasant, when one thinks of all the good and

gracious things that have gone from life since that afternoon, to know that at least this one abomination had gone with them. Among all the modern orgies of law-making, the invention of yet more and more regulations to limit human freedom, there surely could have been some restriction on the cads who torture wild animals in this way. The Hunt kennels are gone from Chipstead and children can no longer wait, as I used to wait for hours, to see the hounds fed, but they are gone because there is no land left to hunt over. That open pursuit of an animal for sport is no more, but the sly, nocturnal trapping which leaves its victims in agonies for hours still persists.

Another horror to me on those afternoon walks would certainly not be inflicted on a child today. This was a meeting with 'the loonies'. Just outside Chipstead was Cane Hill Asylum, then, I think, a charitable or county institution for the insane poor. Once a week or so a party of the women patients would be brought through the lanes by their attendants to the village shop, where they would be allowed to spend a few pennies on sweets. They wore a grey workhouse uniform and walked in a shambling crocodile, grimacing, sometimes skipping or shouting, a terrifying procession to meet. Their modern counterparts are doubtless treated more efficiently, given shock treatment and psycho-analysis and certainly not allowed to buy sweets in a village shop or frighten small children by their antics as they did in Edwardian Chipstead.

[7]

We had our amenities, though. The village hall was used for concerts and occasionally a lantern lecture, but as it was my parents' principle to send their children to bed early I was never present at these.

I did, however, go to the cricket ground and lie in the shade of the great elm trees that surrounded it when one of my elder brothers played for a scratch team captained by young Goad against 'the village'. (Of that team the First World War left only five survivors.) I dare say the occasion was much like a village cricket match today, for this is one thing that remains almost unchanged, but as I remember it, the spectators with parasols or straw hats, the resolute avoidance of a patronising air by the 'gentle-people' on such a democratic occasion, the single motor car near the ground and a dog-cart stopping in the road while its occupants watched for a while, it seems very much of its time and place.

It must have been at the time of the Balkan War that a new craze came to the village. A miniature rifle range was made near Mr. Peckham's cottage and two rifle clubs were formed, one for ladies, who practised in the afternoon, the other for the men at night. It was the time of plays like *An Englishman's Home*, when invasion was more discussed than it was during the war which followed. Firing a ·22 rifle was not only great fun, but an act of patriotism as well. Nobody for a moment seriously thought that war or invasion would ever come, but it was exciting to talk about.

The rifle range brought an unexpected distinction to our household, for my mother turned out to be the best shot in the village and accumulated cups and silver spoons which were kept on a rosewood table in the drawing-room.

That miniature range, a varnished shed with mattresses and a contrivance for bringing back the targets, represented the contemporary attempt to 'Be Prepared'. It was no more ineffectual or pathetic, I suppose, than all that nonsense with gas masks we had before the Second World War. Perhaps it is as well for human dignity that there is nothing much you can do about an atom bomb.

[8]

Even in that stagnant epoch there was change, and during our six years at Chipstead the motor car ceased to be a novelty and became almost commonplace. The surfaces of the roads through the village were not yet adapted to bear the new traffic, though, and were flinted and dusty and cared for only by a solitary roadmender, who wore protected spectacles and pushed a barrow marked with letters to show it was the property of the Rural District Council. He promised me a fossil next time he found one, but either forgot or broke stones without a single fossil in them for several years.

The world beyond our boundaries meant little to us; even the people of Coulsdon (which now touches Chipstead) were foreigners, and at least to me as a child the few lanes which made up our village, each with its discreet houses and gardens, were almost my only sphere.

Public events in the great world were wholly unreal. I remember the sinking of the *Titanic* only because my father told me about it, and the General Election of 1910 because slogans were chalked on the railway bridge and because we wore bits of blue ribbon. I also remember talk of a sort of Corsican ogre who was threatening every patriotic Briton with evil changes and whose name was Lloyd George. My father's wrath at the introduction of compulsory insurance was expressed with violence, but it was all far away to me, who knew as boundaries one road with a line of pines along it, another banked by rhododendrons and a third where wild roses grew.

But some people called Suffragettes suddenly became very real indeed to us, for they set light to the village church. Fortunately, the fire was extinguished before much damage was done, but the incident made a tremendous stir in our community. What was this, our elders asked in 1910, this threat to public security, this violent piece of anarchism, this volcano under them? Suffragettes! They might do anything and no one could consider himself safe from them. Really, one might be back in prehistoric times instead of living in this most enlightened and pacific of all centuries. One local lady was even suspected of being a Suffragette, chiefly because she wore rather virile clothes and had 'radical views' about things. She was not, of course, received by the 'gentle-people'.

But a mightier cataclysm shook the life of Chipstead with the Railway Strike of 1912. To my father and his friends this was not mere folly ('They don't think of their wives and children'), but criminal folly, too, and the work of 'vile Socialists'. As a patriotic Briton, my father supported members of the staff at Chipstead Station and on the line from Purley to Tadworth who remained 'loyal' and today would be called blacklegs. When it was over he raised a subscription among residents up and down the line and collected a considerable sum with which the 'loyal' men were rewarded. They in turn subscribed to give him a souvenir of the occasion, and for some years my father would carry to town the umbrella with which he was presented on their behalf by Mr. Mumford, the Chipstead Stationmaster, who wore a silk hat and gold-braided uniform. I see it as a symbol of the time, no less pathetic and significant than another umbrella became twenty-six years later.

CHAPTER VII

House and Garden

[1]

THE TABLE in the dining-room had a plush cloth of bluish green which fell almost to the floor, so that when I was of table height I could crawl under to make it into a smugglers' cave or an Arab tent. The carpet, on which for me a world was mapped, was a thick-piled Turkey and the chairs were oak with crimson leather seats. There was also a great oak sideboard, from the cupboard of which I would steal lumps of sugar, a cupboard which had a delicious fruity smell when it was opened. Between the table and the fireplace were two armchairs. My parents had bought this furniture expensively in the Tottenham Court Road.

That room must have been pretty hideous, though with none of the gloomy solidity of 'the Emperor's' dining-room at Croydon or the frippery of Grandmother Taylor's at Kingston. Its ugliness was the contemporary one. It was like most things in the first two decades of the century, of no particular school, period or design, it was content *not* to be Victorian.

On the walls were pictures chosen at an art shop either as presents by others or by my parents themselves when they were first furnishing. 'That's rather nice.' 'They'll like *that*.' They were not Highland cattle or swooning ladies, but sensible landscapes or self-explanatory historical scenes, mezzotint engravings in strong oak frames. Pictures were necessary; you could not have all that wall surface without pictures, so 'good taste' had to be used in their selection.

This meant that they must not be extraordinary in any way, or too clever, highly coloured, or startling in theme. Nor, on the other hand, must they be too like the ones everybody else seemed to have, or those met in seaside lodgings. It was not difficult in a good art shop to find pictures which conformed to these standards, and my parents had done so.

That was the keynote of most things in my home—'good taste' rather than taste. The distinction is an important one, and anybody who has been credited with good taste and supposes that it means he has any taste at all is living with illusions. It was and is the very motto of philistinism. All modern art, for instance, and much of the great art of all time fails to satisfy the canons of good taste, while the men who painted it were, in their lives and persons, in the worst possible. All innovation, all unconventionality and most idealism are in poor taste, so is anything like fanaticism or even exaggerated enthusiasm.

Time, it is true, can set the seal of good taste on even the most vehement expressions of human faith, the highest ideologies, but only time, and sometimes a great deal of time, can do it. It took many centuries to make our Lord's teaching acceptable by this standard, and time alone has reconciled to it the earthy realities of Shakespeare. The Victorian age was, of course, the heyday of good taste, as one can see from its architecture now. It was fortunate in having one poet who was always in good taste—Tennyson; unluckily, you could not depend on Browning. Thackeray was perfectly reliable, but Dickens altogether too clamorous of attention for things best left alone.

When it came to Edwardian times, the severity of this was eased a little, particularly in public life dominated by the genial King. Some of the newer writers like Mr. Galsworthy were in excellent taste, though noisy or Fabian persons like H. G. Wells and Bernard Shaw were certainly not. There was a good deal of talk about certain French poets and artists who were supposed to have genius, but how could men who wore eccentric clothes, got drunk on absinthe and led openly scandalous lives be in good taste? Reformers or would-be reformers like Lloyd George and Annie Besant, who wanted to change the world as it was then, were in poor taste, while Christabel Pankhurst, Keir Hardie and General Booth were in such unspeakably bad taste that they could not be mentioned without opprobrium or ridicule, while Oscar Wilde could not be mentioned at all.

Most of the ugliness of the age was attributable to good taste, as that of my home was to my parents. Nothing clashed, nothing was very old, nothing was too modern and nothing really beautiful. Good taste had dictated the choice of the wallpapers, and I can see my parents exercising it as they looked through the book of patterns, marking this or that undistinguished design. The chair-covers, the curtains, the paintwork were all in good taste, all 'went with' the others and the effect was innocuous but commonplace.

In the drawing-room were some rather good watercolours and the flowers were usually plentiful and quite well arranged. My mother's grand piano was never opened when she played, so it was covered by a piece of well-embroidered silk on which stood silver-framed photographs and Worcester china. The cushion-covers were embroidered, too, in sensible designs of flowers in uncompromising colours. The curtains were of a gay chintz, the carpet white with a neat red design, the small tables and chairs of rosewood. There were more personal things. Two porcelain plates, for instance, hung from the wall in invisible wire frames. Their design of tulips had actually been painted by my mother before they went to the enamelling furnace, for she had taken a course of pottery while 'finishing' in Paris. Then a huge photograph album with thick cardboard pages, silk endpapers, gilt edges and a gilt clasp held photographs of members of both my parents' families. There were also some pieces of porcelain of the period, a few small silver objects, a little modern gilt clock, a pair of three-branched silver candlesticks and my mother's work-basket—nothing, it will be observed, in the least exotic or eccentric.

Yet that was in its way a pleasant room, certainly a cheerful one. Its lattice windows opened on the garden and the sun poured in at noon and my mother played her piano on most mornings. I liked to be in the drawing-room.

[2]

My parents' bedroom was even more of the period, if that is possible. It was dominated by a huge brass bedstead which had a high headpiece with hinged wings from which hung curtains of glazed chintz. An eiderdown was on it, not one of the puffed-up slippery eiderdowns of today, but one quilted in small divisions and larger than the surface of the bed.

On a table beside this brazen erection was a spirit stove for making early morning tea and a box of Plasman biscuits. Over it was a large photograph of my mother's father in a frame of stained oak with a gilt design on it. The dressing-table had my mother's set of silver-backed brushes, a pin-cushion and china box for hair-tidies and hairpins.

The whole room is impregnated in my memory with the scent of the lotion my father always used for his hair, but it was called hair-wash, not lotion, then. It came from 'the Stores'. (To us 'the Stores', *tout court*, meant the Civil Service Supply Association. The Army and Navy Stores was 'the Army and Navy', while Selfridges had not been long enough established to be patronised.) This hair-wash was of a pale brown colour, and frothed when you shook the bottle, as you were instructed to do. It was called *Rosemary, Bay Rum and Cantharidine Hair-wash* and it had no oil in it, but a pleasant fresh smell which to me is the smell of that age.

My own bedroom I remember only as the place in which I was ill. It was usually my father who would make the discovery—'that child looks very flushed'—and Ninna would fetch the thermometer. It if showed a temperature above normal, it set in motion a good deal of activity.

Influenza in its milder forms was a family ailment and a slight temperature with a head cold was diagnosed as 'flu. I would be popped—invariable word—into bed with a vast earthenware hot-water bottle. Ninna would put a nightlight and a hand-bell in the room in case I needed anything during the night. If I had a sore throat she would add a remedy of her own, butter mixed with sugar, of which I was told not to take too much at a time. A paraffin stove would be lit and brought in, and I can still see the pattern on the ceiling made by its light shining through the holes in its top. If I grew worse, Dr. Tudge would be sent for, and I remember him as a rather solemn young man who, my father said, was a 'very clever chap'. (Other doctors were described sweepingly as 'no good at all'.)

Things which invariably accompanied 'flu were milk-and-soda, rusks, beef tea and calf's-foot jelly. The happiest time was during convalescence, when I could sit up, have my toys or later books, but not get up for two days after the temperature had returned to normal nor go out for two days more.

Only once did my father have this 'flu and that made him the centre of a hushed but happy whirl. A coal fire was hastily and silently lit in the little-used grate in his room, the blinds drawn to give him enough light without worrying his eyes, while beside him were set Things He Might Want —milk, a siphon, rusks, barley water, medicines, newspapers and the thermometer. In the afternoon visiting cards were slipped in the letter-box, though no bell was inconsiderately rung, and each had the solemn message, 'To enquire', written on it.

My father soon recovered, but from *Mrs Beeton's Book of Household Management* of 1910 may be gathered what would have been the measures taken if he had grown worse. Orders would scarcely have been given for straw to be laid in the road outside to deaden the sound of horses' hoofs, though I, and I am sure many living people, can remember seeing a few yards of a street under a thick bed of straw. ('Someone's very ill,' said Ninna with awe.) A trained nurse would certainly have been sent for and paid the contemporary fee of two guineas a week. 'Anything,' says Mrs Beeton 'that can be done to while away the long hours of weakness should be tried, whether it be reading aloud or by the nurse engaging herself with some occupation that it would be pleasant for the invalid to watch.' No suggestions are made about this occupation, so one is left wondering whether the nurse was expected to turn cart-wheels or merely do some good conjuring tricks. None of us, however, needed a trained nurse after my mother's last *accouchement*.

[3]

A flight of narrow stairs led from the landing to the servants' bedroom, which I was forbidden to enter, and the attic, which was a delightful place. It was a long room directly under the eaves of the house and had a small window at one end. It was full of trunks, bags and those vast basket crates used by laundries for their largest deliveries. These held a miscellany of old dress materials, pieces of curtain, outmoded clothes of my mother's, old empty ledgers of unknown origin, some harness kept from the days of the dog-cart, plumage from long-ago hats, ornamental buttons removed from discarded clothes, badminton shuttlecocks and racquets, a pair of skates, a riding-crop, some lace, horse blankets with my father's initials on them, and, rather mysteriously, a stethoscope.

Such a collection would be a challenge to the ingenuity of any child and I took advantage of it. I spent long hours in that low, stuffy room with its scent of clothes stored with lavender and of timber hot under the slates, for here were all the props necessary for a dozen forms of make-believe. My entertainment was solitary, for the three years' difference made me too young for my older brothers, too old for my younger. I was then and throughout my boyhood happiest when I was alone, though no grown-ups understood this. So I rode to York or navigated tropical seas under a horse-blanket sail, became snakily Red Indian with an ostrich-feather head-dress or visited the sick-beds of the suffering with the still inexplicable stethoscope.

One day I made a discovery which gave to all this a new reality. The landing, the servants' bedroom and a store-cupboard formed a straight-sided, flat-roofed section set in the middle of the space under the eaves, and the attic I knew was between this cube and the slope of the roof. Behind the store-cupboard was a way through to an identical area on the other side, but this had been concealed by boxes because no flooring had been laid and it was considered that anyone crawling along there might damage the lath and plaster between the beams.

I first discovered this way through on a bright winter morning. Peering down the narrow tunnel I could see light at the far end. I think that was one of the most enthralling moments I have known, for it meant nothing less than a secret passage to a secret room. Surely no one has so far forgotten childhood that he cannot sense the ecstasy in that.

The journey through the triangular tunnel was a painful one, a long crawl over the rough timber of the beams. But, emerging, I found that it was true: a room was there with a window, but no door, a room identical in size and shape with the box-room I had left, but without floorboards or means of access for anybody but a child. I instantly convinced myself that I was the first human being to enter it.

I sat there on the uncomfortable beams and tried to realise it. I needed no make-believe now; however much this suggested the state-room of a captured galleon or the secret lair of a bandit, however perfect it would have been as a castle hall, the reality was better, a secret room which only I could enter, of whose existence only I knew.

My plans were practical. Provisions must be obtained, a candle and matches and perhaps a few things from the neighbouring box-room brought through. I anticipated spending a great deal of time here and should be prepared for siege. The provisions I meant were not those advertised over grocers' shops, but the provisions of romance, provisions for a voyage or an overland trek.

But all plans were suddenly defeated. Ninna came up to the box-room to call me for lunch and, not finding me, looked round the room and saw the boxes moved from the entrance to the tunnel. She was calling me to come at once. I made my slow way back and was told to look at my clothes all covered in dust, and those knees! I had no business to go crawling about, and now I should be late for lunch.

Before I could take that way again the entrance had been closed, not with movable boxes, but securely by a carpenter with matchboarding.

For years afterwards I used to think of the secret room, existing there out of human knowledge, unvisited by anything larger than mice. Somehow its window, through which nobody looked out to the garden beneath, gave it a certain uncanniness, as though it might have silent and insubstantial visitors at times. Even today as I sit writing on the terrace of a villa overlooking the sunlit city of Tangier nearly half a century later I feel a faint touch of the old sense of mystery. Has it ever been unboarded, I wonder? Has it perhaps been made part of the house? Or is it still there for a small boy to find and possess in secret? Against me that paradise was quickly closed, but perhaps others have been more fortunate and realised my plans or their own. I hope so. There cannot be many secret rooms under the eaves of modern houses.

[4]

In all this catalogue of the contents of a house, it may have been noticed, there has been no mention made of books. The only books at Wayside were in a small bookshelf in the dining-room which, with most of its contents, had been taken over with the house. They were chiefly novels, I remember, some by a certain Mary Broughton, whose work I have never come on again, even when I kept a second-hand bookshop.

When, under the persuasion of Miss Wain, I had reached the stage of reading for pleasure, I tried to struggle through some of these novels and failed until I came on a book called *Barbary Sheep*, by Robert Hichens. This delighted me and I still remember a character, vaguely sheik-like, who attracted an Englishwoman's attention by cracking nuts between two fingers, and soon after, meeting her in a lonely place, hid her under his burnous on the approach of some of her compatriots in order to save her good name. What else he did I cannot say, because my mother found me absorbed in the book and immediately confiscated it.

'Not *at all* the sort of book for a little boy to read,' I was told.

Perhaps to correct the harm done by Mr. Hichens, my father brought down from the City two bound volumes of *Chums* of earlier years, and thereafter I did not lack reading-matter. My contemporaries will remember the small type

and grey-yellow paper over which we pored, the world well
lost and time forgotten. The serials had alliterative titles—
The Mystery of Melford Manor, I remember, and *The Spy at
Sedgemere School*. It was like cheating to be able to turn at
once to the next instalment, not to have the intolerable wait
for another week which subscribers to the periodical had.
It was almost too exciting to bear when a schoolboy, whose
father was believed to have been lost with all hands on a
ship called the *Kraken*, bought a parrot which repeated

> Billy Tarr of the Calabar,
> Gone where the *Kraken* and the dead men are,
> And dead men tell no tales,

and recognised in this a clue to the mystery, a clue which he
was able to follow to a triumphant reunion.

Otherwise the only books at Wayside were childish
picture books soon scorned, my mother's cookery books
and bound copies of *The Stock Exchange Year-book*, in which
my father's name could be found in print.

[5]

Wayside was a garden house with flower-beds under all
its windows and a terrace behind it open to the tennis
court, a house entirely surrounded by lawns and borders.
In its garden as I look back I see the weaknesses and the
achievements of contemporary gardening and of my father
as a gardener.

Those were still the days of 'bedding out' and 'rustic
work'. Cheap labour made fine lawns, grass verges, crammed herbaceous borders and a never-ceasing succession of
flowers for the house fairly easy to maintain. But there was
little overall design discernible and no attempt to produce
good vistas or to make the most of the shape and setting,

or to produce splendid massed effects. Flowering shrubs were delegated to take their chance in crowded 'shrubberies' and nothing like a 'feature' of stone or water was found.

The front door of the house looked out on a small lawn, while to the left was the front gate surrounded by a shrubbery designed to shield the house for as long as possible from those entering. The shrubbery was an interesting place for a child to crawl into, but had little to recommend it to eye—a laburnum, cotoneasters and holly bushes. But behind that small lawn was a deep herbaceous border running back to a thick, high hedge, and that border was superb. The front of it had been made to curve simply and naturally behind the lawn, the edge of which was kept clipped sharply. First came an edging of pale mauve violas, which my father preferred to variegated pansies, and behind them were patches of fairly short-stemmed annuals and bedded-out greenhouse plants—salpiglossis, clarkia, godetia, nigella, antirrhinums, zinnias, petunias and the rest. The middle distance was of lupins, phlox, gaillardias, pyrethrums, while behind, of course, were great blazing blue stems of the delphiniums, massed marguerites, Michaelmas daisies, heleniums and rudbeckias.

That mixed border was part of a garden of more than one acre in extent maintained by one gardener and a lad, yet it remained full of colour for six months of the year. I remember the yellow calceolarias which were brought out from the greenhouse, the feathery asters and the proud hollyhocks behind them all. Dahlias my father grew among the rest of his plants, not separately for cutting, and even, mistakenly, I think, included gladioli in his mixture.

He bought most of his half-hardy annuals from nurserymen and was always impatient for delivery. I can remember standing with him before boxes of plants in a Purley shop while he gave a never-ceasing order and the nurseryman wrote busily. Balsam, ageratum, cosmea, nemesia, stocks, boxes of them were to be delivered without fail on the following day. Assurances were given by the nurseryman and as my father paid he said characteristically, 'If you don't send them over tomorrow, I'll never deal with you again.' How intolerable it sounds today, but it only brought yet another assurance from the nurseryman.

I dare say most of the flowers my father grew in that border have been improved since then, have been crossed or grafted, pollinated or hybridised, cross-fertilised or budded, till they are scarcely recognisable. Certainly the delphiniums of today would dwarf his finest, aquilegias have spurs twice as long and lupins are in a score of new colours. Many of the scents of that border have gone as the size and colour of plants have improved, and many new plants of great beauty have become popular which were then unknown. Yet it was no small achievement and rather in advance of its time. Horticulture in England had left 200 years before the stern formality of the Italian garden, with geometrically shaped beds and trees cut to artificial shapes, had passed through the age of Capability Brown, when great vistas of parkland were created, but had not yet emerged from the Victorian vogue for flower beds set in lawns in which a succession of flowers were bedded out. My father's herbaceous border was not unique, of course, was not even very original, but it was looked on as something of a bold innovation at the time.

Away to the right of this was the rose garden, and here my father's fondness for rustic work and Dorothy Perkins rambler roses had quite run amok. The design was formal—four oblong beds with paths between them and in the centre a circle. But the central paths ran under arches of rustic work smothered in that viciously overgrowing, blatantly blooming rambler and the central circle had rustic work all round it which rose to a point in the centre so that we called it 'the bandstand'. This also was crushed under the embraces of Dorothy Perkins.

Yet the roses in the beds, which were called bush roses then, not hybrid tea, were fine, well-chosen and well grown. The beds were planned to be narrow enough to make all the bushes accessible from the path and between those bushes my father always grew sweet alyssum, covering the ground with a white carpet which was edged with dark blue lobelia. In every garden he made, this was repeated; rose-beds carpeted with alyssum and edged with dwarf lobelia.

The garden was divided into pieces by high laurel hedges, one of which ran behind the tennis court, another from the house to the rose garden. There was an orchard divided from the tennis court by a gravel path under an arch of rustic work and Dorothy Perkins. This led to the kitchen garden.

Here was order, here was plenty. The permanent bed of strawberries was covered in its season by old fishing-nets on posts to keep out the birds, but occasionally an unlucky blackbird would get in by some hole or tear in the netting and be pursued, caught and released, with shrill cries from itself and from us. The asparagus bed, the raspberry canes, the little rows of black and white currant bushes and the gooseberry bushes, all were planned with precision. Across the gravel path were the vegetables themselves in lines like well-drilled soldiers, not a potato out of place.

[6]

I must have spent more of my life in that garden than in any area of its size anywhere. For six years I was rarely out of it for a day, except when I was at boarding school. I could draw a plan of it now, for all its intricate divisions.

For me, more than a garden, more than an example of Edwardian horticulture, it was a place of remembered experiences.

I discovered, for instance, that by turning a metal wheelbarrow upside down, sitting on it and spinning the wheel before me I could become a pioneer aviator, rising through the trees of the orchard and making long voyages into space. I might even have crossed the Channel, as M. Blériot had done that very summer, if I had the least idea what to expect on the other side. That wheelbarrow kept me happy for a whole August afternoon—and how long an afternoon was when one was six years old—but I could not go back to it, I remember. Turning it over a few days later, I found that after all it was nothing but an inverted wheelbarrow and would no longer rise from the grass.

Reading in some boys' magazines a way to trap birds in a gin made with four bricks and baited with grain, I set one of these up one day and found it hideously successful. But when I found that all I could do with the bird once caught was to free it—for then as now I have a fastidious dislike of taking life, even insect life—I found the whole thing rather pointless and abandoned it. Nor did I ever crave for an airgun or catapult. I tried several times to bring up young birds, feeding them with a matchstick on ground birdseed and milk, but never with success.

What distances there seemed to be in that garden. I remember it as a long walk from the front gate at the top to the rubbish-heap at the bottom, a walk which might be broken anywhere by some event or spectacle, or sudden impulse. One day the elm trees which ran down one side of it were cut back to mere branchless blocks but, although forbidden to approach, I could watch from the orchard. Once there was a strange man working in the garden whom I was not allowed to talk to because he was believed to be a little bit 'funny', which meant either mentally deficient or tipsy.

I had a passionate craving of an almost mystical kind in some way to go into the earth, and remember lying at full length contemplating a small hole in the ground under the laurel bushes, longing to shrink like Alice to a size to enter it. When therefore my father decided that a new and much larger cesspool should be dug in a part of the garden far from the old one, I watched with envy while men dug their way downwards. At last I persuaded them to let me make the journey down the shaft in the bucket with which one was hauling up the loose clay, and this was a great adventure.

On summer nights in the garden my parents would suddenly decree that I might sleep out and Ninna would make up a camp-bed on the lawn. I could smell the heliotrope in the border and see the bats overhead and know a happiness quite new to me as I lay on my back and looked up at the stars without interruption.

But there were disillusionments too. Beyond the tennis court and laurel hedge was a small piece of lawn used in turn by us for croquet, clock-golf and a game called bumble-puppy, for which there was a sudden craze at the time. Beside this lawn was a water-butt, and the gardener, a facetious man, told me to come to it after tea that day, when he would show me a water otter he had caught for me. I knew about otters from a book of beasts and they sounded enchanting creatures with webbed feet, thick whiskers and small eyes who lived in streams and brought up their young in grass nests. I bolted my tea and rushed to the water-butt. There was the gardener holding a line of which one end was in the water. When he began to draw on this my excitement was painful.

It was a joke. A kettle arrived at the surface. 'A water 'otter, see?' laughed the gardener. 'Didn't I tell you I'd got a water 'otter?' I did not forgive him and if he is alive he remains unforgiven by me. I have still never seen an otter.

Each of us was given a garden of his own and a few pence to go to 'Philipses' and buy seed, with strong advice to concentrate on nasturtiums, which gave quick returns. I insisted—I can only suppose the names attracted me—on Love-lies-bleeding and Love-in-a-mist, and both came up in profusion, as they have done in any garden I have made since, as they do even in Tangier.

[7]

My father, like most people of his class and background, was an enthusiastic, one might almost say a rabid, royalist and planned to celebrate the Coronation of King George V with considerable display. He detested and distrusted fireworks ('Most dangerous things. You might blow your eye out') and did not love noise of any kind, so the show was to be chiefly a visual one.

For it he ordered 500 glass night-lights, like inverted rough tumblers, in red, white and blue glass. These had wire attachments and were to be hung round the garden from trees or rustic arches. Then a brass band would play and my father and his guests would drink the King's health and there would be a buffet on the lawn.

This was all very well, but took no account of English weather. On the night of the Coronation, June 22nd, 1911, it began to rain as the whole household was marshalled to light the 500 night-lights, and the *fête champêtre* had to be abandoned. This was lucky for me as I was away at school at the time and my father, not to be outdone or waste his 500 coloured glasses, postponed his party till August.

I remember the occasion better than the Coronations which have come since. They gathered, my father's friends, the nice people of Chipstead, the nice families who had remained friends from previous homes of ours, the nice friends from the Stock Exchange, for it was an occasion to show loyalty to the Crown, to exhibit their faith in the continuance of things as they were and incidentally to pass a pleasant and mildly unusual evening with plenty to eat and drink.

It was a warm summer night and the coloured lights made a brave show in red, white and blue. The band played patriotic airs and it seems in memory that a large concourse of people strolled about the gravel paths and across the lawns and ate in a small marquee. The Taylors were in force and the Cooke aunts, Eirene and Xenia, grey and black night birds in shawls.

The men, I remember, talked violently of what they would like to do with Asquith, who was accused of 'dragging in the King' to secure the passage of the Parliament Act to abolish the veto of the House of Lords, a disgraceful and disturbing business which had come to a head that week. But it did not spoil the evening or modify their celebration of the new reign's beginning, or harm the plentiful champagne.

[8]

I was just eight years old, so it will sound a little whimsical if I say I fell in love that night, but the expression is often used with less justification. A family had come to live on a new road down to the station taking a biggish house for the parents and grown-up daughters and almost grown-up sons. My father strongly approved of them ('Very decent sort of people'), and all of them came to the Coronation party. It was one of the daughters, a girl of nineteen or twenty, I suppose, who enchanted me.

She was wearing a cream-coloured dress and she had a rich, kind voice. She made friends with me and asked me to show her the garden and we walked about together. Looking back now, I cannot remember her face, but her physical presence is vivid, her scent, her clothes, her nearness, her little, quiet laugh. She did not patronise me or laugh at me; she was warmly and inspiringly friendly.

I talked more and more and was afraid she would go back to the others. We met my mother, and she asked the girl if I was boring her and the girl said no, and we wandered away again. It was a tremendous moment for me—I had made a grown-up friend, the first in my life. In an impetuous moment of confidence, I asked if she would like to see *my* garden, the square of ground thick with Love-lies-bleeding and Love-in-a-mist. She said she would and we went down to it. I remember her standing there in near-darkness away from the 500 lights and talking about gardening. I do not remember going back to the others or anything else of the evening, just the cream-coloured figure near my little patch of garden, the kindness, the nearness, the warmth and the pride.

A week later the family was joining ours for a picnic at Kingswood. We were to call for them, walk down to the station and go by train to the next stop. We had not reached the station before I desolately knew that it was over. She was one with the grown-ups. Either the wonder of that evening in the garden had been entirely created by my imagination or she had forgotten it. She certainly could not be bothered with me. One of her brothers was a 'funny man' and she was playing up to him. There was a great deal of laughter in the train and I was heartbroken.

[9]

Neither house nor garden seem to me in retrospect to have changed much during our six years in them. The garden was improved, but kept the general plan it had when we arrived, for my father had no gift for design on anything but a small scale. The house changed its wallpapers and chintzes, no doubt, but nothing more radical. There was nothing unusual in this conservatism, for in those days people kept their homes much as they were. There was no professional interior decorating and far less interest in antique furniture, fabrics, lighting and the rest.

Wayside was lit by paraffin lamps in iron brackets high on the walls. These lamps were taken out to the kitchen each day to be cleaned and refilled. The house was heated by coal fires in the kitchen, dining-room and nursery—that in the drawing-room was 'laid', but only lit when it was wanted. I doubt if any house in Chipstead had central heating or any means of cooking except the kitchen range. No vacuum-cleaner droned, but there was a thing called a carpet-sweeper with circular brushes in a box—this was pushed to and fro by the housemaid. Water for the bathroom was heated by opening a damper in the kitchen range, and could only provide one bath in two hours.

Worse, the floors had stained floorboards round the carpets, and the lino in the kitchen and bathroom was called 'oilcloth'. Table knives were cleaned by the gardener's boy on a knife-board with Wellington knife-powder, which displayed the Iron Duke's head on its tins. Milk was delivered in a metal tin which had been filled from a large brass churn in the milk-float driven from house to house, and the milkman called 'Milk-O!' when he approached the back door. No one had heard of a refrigerator, nobody used a cigarette-lighter, washing-machine or electric iron. The 'mangle' which stood in the gardener's shed was

enormous. Tooth paste was unheard of in our household—
Carbolic Tooth Powder being invariably used. There was
nearly half an acre of lawn at Wayside, but no one had
thought of a motor-mower.

In spite of these and other primitive customs, we con-
trived to have leisure, contentment and health. It will seem
odd to members of a modern household whose comfort,
entertainment and well-being are maintained by television,
radio, electricity, refrigeration, gas, central heating, the
health service, the telephone, the motor car, air transport,
mass production, D.D.T., radar, penicillin and atomic
energy that we managed to be happy with none of those
things.

CHAPTER VIII

Journeys and Holidays

[1]

NOBODY LIVING in Chipstead before the First World War owned a motor car, I think, and there was no local taxi. To leave the village, everyone walked to the station (or in wet weather took a fly) and went by train.

Except for summer holidays, when for a month or two our entire household moved to a furnished house by the sea, the only places outside Chipstead with which I was at all familiar were Croydon and Purley. To these I was taken by my mother for visits to the dentist or hairdresser.

I went to London once or twice, but only to be hurried from one station to another. I knew the pungent smell of a brewery passed as the train came in, the cobbles of the station yard noisy with the hoofs of cab-horses, the frightening streets crowded with horse-traffic and an intensity, a high-pitched sense of impending crisis which I always felt as a small boy when I was taken up to Town.

But visits to Croydon and Purley were delightful and even the dentist could not spoil them, for the pain he inflicted was to be compensated by a treat afterwards. The barber's shop was made interesting by the extraordinary machinery overhead. This unhygienic device, which has disappeared from the premises of modern hairdressers, consisted of a bar with large wheels, round each of which was a double rubber band. When he had finished cutting my hair the barber would ask if I wanted the brush and when I eagerly assented he would put a huge circular brush in the other end of the looped rubber band and set the thing in whirring motion so that the bristles would spin over my head most excitingly.

I rode on trams in Croydon and Purley and knew the stops—Swan and Sugar-loaf and Greyhound. I went with my mother to shop at Alders and chose a cap-pistol promised me as a treat after a painful hour at the dentist's. Then we would go to Bramley Hill to tea at 'the Emperor's'.

That was the best part of the day for me. 'The Emperor' himself would not leave his study till tea-time and my mother and I would be greeted by my Aunt Eirene. But presently would come the summons for me, and I would go alone to the old gentleman's room and, as instructed, knock.

He would be standing on his hearth-rug and look down with his aloof smile. He was so kind and friendly to me, so patient in explaining things, so willing to show me trea-sures, that I find it hard to reconcile my memories of him with the stories told by his own children. Once he showed me a book printed in black letter.

'That,' he said, 'was one of the first books printed in England. It was printed by William Caxton. Have you heard of him?'

By chance I had and it pleased 'the Emperor'.

'He was born in Kent. You were born in Kent, too, were you not?'

Then out would come the Alva plums or Chinese figs or the piece of *chocolat*. Or it would be time to go through to the hushed and gloomy dining-room, where tea would be laid on a cloth at the large table and we would sit round it with solemnity, the gas jet wheezing overhead. The tea-service was ornamented with the crest of 'the Emperor's' college and there was always blackberry jam.

The return journey would be made from Purley Station

and I can hear the porters shouting on the approach of our train—'Reedham, Smitham, Chipstead, Kingswood and Tadworth.' There was another list with which they heralded trains that went to alien places like Burgh Heath, but *our* list I can hear as clearly as the words being shouted now from the tower of a neighbouring mosque.

[2]

My father had never been to the theatre as a child and saw no need for children to have that sort of entertainment now. Besides, he believed that infection was passed when people were crowded together. 'You catch all sorts of awful diseases in those places,' he said. My mother, who as a girl had joined many theatre parties of the gregarious Taylors and had been present at the first night of *The Mikado*, occasionally persuaded my father to let her take us to some entertainment, but I was only in a theatre once during my first fourteen years, and that was to see a Christmas pantomime at Croydon.

I suppose this, or something like it, must be the first experience of most of us, but children who have been accustomed to going to the cinema since they have been able to walk cannot know all the magic of one's first time in a theatre, when even the gilt plaster and mural paintings seem ethereal and to wait for the curtain to go up becomes an agony.

It was *Cinderella*; the opening chorus was in the market-place and when it was over I thought we must have reached the end of the performance. Surely one could not be given *more* of such stupendously beautiful sight and sound, light and colour and loveliness? But there was a Baron and a Buttons who sang a song together which I have never heard since or seen among contemporary collections—

'I don't suppose we'll do it again
For months, and months, and months.'

it went on, that wonderful pantomime for an eternity, but I
must have been sated by its splendours, for I can remember
no more, or the return home, or talking about it afterwards.

On another occasion, which would have been in 1909, I
think, my mother took us all to the Crystal Palace. This was
a treat, an outing, an excursion and very much an adventure.
The gardens then were a pleasure park, not quite a fairground raucous with mechanical music, nor much like the
pleasure gardens of a century earlier, but something between
the two. The amusements offered were less blatant and on a
weekday the crowds less dense than those of modern fair-
grounds.

We went in swing-boats and on a helter-skelter; we
wandered, a somewhat forlorn little party, my mother,
Ninna, my younger brothers and I, among attractions so
various and beguiling that it was difficult for us to know
how best to spend the money—a sovereign, I suspect—
which my father had given my mother for the day. We
decided to go into the Magic Tunnel, because you sat in a
little boat on real water and were carried gently by the
stream into 'caverns measureless to man, Down to a sunlit
sea'. As you drifted through the half-darkness you arrived,
every few moments, at illuminated scenes by the stream-
side, brightly lit caverns or fairy castles and it was sad to
emerge to reality and the light of day.

We had brought our lunch and picnicked among the
stone reproductions of prehistoric mammals, unfriendly-
looking pelycosaur and brontosaurus, horrid titanothere and
monstrous trachodon. In the afternoon we decided rashly
to spend the last of our money on entering the Haunted
House and marched in a body past the white skeleton which
shook and rattled just inside the door. There were screams

K

and horrors ahead, currents of whistling air, chains clank-
ing in the darkness, a gibbet with a figure hanging from it,
such delicious and macabre things that I was in ecstasy. But
for my little brothers it was too much, and my mother had to
call from a window to the attendants to come and take us
out. This caused a sensation among the crowd, but was a
splendid advertisement for the hauntedness of the house.

Tired with the long day's pleasures, we went up to the
glass building itself to rest on a terrace outside the concert
hall. Then suddenly my mother and Ninna became excited
for the first time that day, for Madame Patti was to sing and
there was a small window open.

I was six years old and no ardent musician, but sensitive
to emotion in those near me. Some of what my mother and
Ninna felt communicated itself to me and I stared down the
hall from our open window and saw, far away on a great
stage among hot-house ferns and plants a tiny white figure.

'Hush,' said Ninna, but there was no need to tell me that.
I did not want to speak or move. I heard the magical sounds
which meant so much to grown-ups and was caught up in a
kind of intoxication.

'Madame Patti!' gasped Ninna after one item, 'Adelina
Patti! We've heard Madame Patti!'

And I can say it now, for what it is worth. Of course no
musical recollection remains to me—how could it? I remember only the awe and rapture of listening to something
which held even grown-ups spellbound.

Then, and this clearly I remember, the little figure spoke.
From the centre of the stage she looked, as it seemed,
directly at us.

'Now I am going to sing you *The Last Rose of Summer*,'
she said and was at once applauded.

I suppose it is the penalty of being a writer, dedicated to
words and people rather than to notes and instruments, that
I can remember how I felt, I can remember the sight of

Patti and the words she spoke, but have no recollection at all of her voice except that it seemed very beautiful to me. But those tired moments on the terrace after the long day's unwonted pleasures and the sudden electrification produced by the name of Patti, make a precious memory. 'And did you once see Shelley plain?' I must be one of the very few of my generation who have heard what older critics still assure us was the loveliest soprano voice in human memory and, some believe, of all time. She was sixty-six that year, and although her last public appearance was not until five years later when she sang to raise funds for the Red Cross after the outbreak of war, this was her last tour in England.

[3]

Every summer, after long preparations, we would move as a household to the seaside, my father having rented a furnished house or furnished rooms in one of the South Coast towns. Surely only in England could there have grown up anything quite like these watering-places with solid Victorian architecture and always 'a nice part of the town' and one 'full of trippers'. The very names of these twin places show the sharp division between gentility and vulgarity—Hastings and St. Leonards-on-Sea, Brighton and Hove, Margate and Cliftonville, and so on. Needless to say, our quarters were always in the more refined and far less interesting regions.

What an institution was the family holiday of those days. The great hampers from the attic had to be packed and sent off in advance, then, on the day, a brake was hired to take us all to the station, for it was a journey to the seaside then, not a run down the road in a car. There was the first glimpse of the sea from the train window, the arrival at the house and

exploration of it, the first approach to the sea itself. Thereafter came the long days of making sand-castles, the donkey
rides, the shrimp teas, the nigger minstrels. We always
bathed in the early morning, for some reason, and came
hungry to breakfast. I never had enough of the sand, the
rocks, the water, shrimping-nets and buckets. I could not
bear to know that the holiday was coming to an end and
that soon I should be catching a last glimpse of the sea as so
recently I had caught the first.

But the seaside family holiday was a strictly middle-class
institution, and the beaches and promenades of St.
Leonards-on-Sea or Cliftonville were never polluted by the
presence of the proletariat. Small shopkeepers, clerks and
other white-collar workers could sometimes manage a week
in August, but they would remain in the lower end of the
town. The 'nice end' was populated by 'gentle-people'.

We did not always stay in a town, for the first holiday I
remember was spent at Pevensey Bay, then a few houses not
far from the isolated small village of Pevensey. A muddle
of history and architecture remains to me of it, the huge
castle walls and the landing of William the Conqueror
confused with something about smugglers. This, touched
by the salt chill of jumping about in a rough sea before
the sun was up.

Another year we were far from a town, at Cooden Beach,
for my father had rented one of the half-dozen cottages
which were then the place's only human habitations. I
remember chiefly the well from which we had to draw our
water.

The most memorable holiday was spent at Clacton, then
a pleasant and peaceful little town. 'The Emperor' came to
stay with us, for the house which my father had taken was a
large one. It belonged to some people vaguely known to
have lived abroad a lot. There were horribly realistic stuffed
lizards and the main room of the house was on two levels,

with two steps between, which seemed to me an interesting and novel arrangement.

'The Emperor' bought me a kite and not only showed me how to fly it, but gave me strange and miscellaneous information about kite-flying from which I remember only that the Chinese were the world's oldest kite-fliers.

'The Germans call it a dragon,' he said, but I have no idea what he meant by that.

He also invited me one morning to prepare myself, as he was taking me out somewhere. I trotted beside him to a confectioner's and there he bought me the first ice-cream of my life, a pink and in retrospect infinitely delicious affair. My father disapproved of ready-made confectionery of most kinds ('You never know what rubbish they put in those things'), and I might have reached maturity without knowing what ice-cream was if it had not been for 'the Emperor'.

Another seaside holiday was spent at Seaford in a house where chickens were kept. That was memorable for two days of unclouded glory. On one my father had decided to walk to Alfriston, four miles away, and, when I was seeing him off with my mother, he suddenly asked me if I thought I could walk four miles, and took me with him. It was almost the only occasion of childhood when I was alone with my father for a whole day, conversing and laughing man to man. We had lunch at an old inn in the main street which had two carved figures guarding its door, and my father went to the bar for a pint of ale before we went to the little dining-room upstairs.

The other great day was when a Mr. Jefferies, who had been my father's clerk on the Stock Exchange and was now a partner in another firm, came down and took us out prawning. We went to the mouth of the Cuckmere River and found the whole foreshore deserted. We let down our nets and returned to pull them up by their floating corks attached to cords and it seemed that there were always prawns in them. Or is Time at its trick of idealisation again? Anyhow, there was wind and sunlight and a deserted beach and the wild excitement of drawing up the nets and finding the great grey prawns.

Another holiday at Kingsgate, for which the house was shared with one of the Taylor uncles and his family, I have chronicled in my novel, *Fall of Man*, with no exaggeration of the hearty *bonhomie* of my Uncle Horace. There were also holidays at Cliftonville and Ramsgate, and all the Thanet coast seemed then a place of legend, haunted by smugglers, Excisemen and the ghosts of Barham's characters. It was, in fact, more like the *Ingoldsby* Thanet than the teeming, cacophonous coach terminus of today.

[4]

When any of us had been ill it was usually decided to 'pack him off' to Annie Dickson at St. Leonards-on-Sea. Mine is by no means the only family then or today with the good fortune to possess an elderly and hospitable relative who lives in a watering-place and is always ready to take one of the children for a week or two after an illness. I know many others who have grown up with their obligations to an aunt in Bournemouth or a distant cousin living in Torquay. But I cannot believe that any was better fitted for it than dear, good, simple Annie Dickson.

She was not strictly speaking an aunt, for she was my mother's cousin, but that was never even understood by us, for whom she was always Auntie Annie. So dependable, so immovable was the whole institution known to us as 'Auntie Annie's' that I find it hard to believe that she is not still there behind the lace curtains in De Champ Road, St. Leonards, waiting for one of us to be sufficiently recovered from 'flu to come down and spend a convalescence with her and Emma, the servant who remained with her for thirty years.

In appearance she looked and dressed rather like the late Queen Mary, though her bearing was not regal. That appearance never changed as far as I could see from my first stay with her in 1909 till her death in her seventies in 1930. She was static, not dynamic. She was a staunch Protestant and, though the kindest of women, always spoke with forced ferocity about Papists. There was a Jesuit Seminary at Hastings and I once heard Auntie Annie, who would never have hurt a fly, wish that the Zeppelin which dropped some bombs in the region had hit it. An only daughter, she had lived alone with her mother for many years, and after my Great-aunt Dickson's death kept the house exactly as it had been, and with Emma and another servant lived in quiet comfort and plenty. Her pleasures were to attend St. Matthew's, the most sternly evangelical of the local churches, twice every Sunday, to have tea at Addison's once or twice a week, to 'listen to the band' occasionally and to exchange daily but always formal visits with her lifelong friends, the Misses Spiers, who lived up the road.

Day would start with morning prayers in the dining-room. Auntie Annie would sit beside the table on which the breakfast was getting cold and read a chapter of the Bible to Emma, the housemaid and me when I was staying with her. Then we all knelt at our chairs and said the Our Father before we could attack the boiled eggs which were waiting under little woollen egg-cosies. A Conservative as uncompromisingly as she was a Protestant, she would ask me to read her the leading article in the *Daily Mail* after breakfast and nod approval of all the harsher things said about Mr. Lloyd George and the Liberals. Then she went out to the kitchen for her discussion of domestic details with Emma, before going upstairs to put on the archaic, heavy-looking coat and hat which she wore to go shopping. We would set out for the tram stop, from which we would make the creaking and groaning tram journey to the Memorial, the clock tower in the centre of Hastings.

She did not talk much, for she had, almost literally, nothing to say. But she smiled often and understood things about children which few grown-ups understand, such as the absolute necessity of being the one to hand the conductor the two pennies and hold the tickets, the importance of counting the paces between lamp-posts and the delirious pleasure of sitting in Cave's Oriental Café and choosing from a plate of fancy cakes that which one wanted most. Everyone knows that a child likes cakes, but it is only inspired grown-ups like my Auntie Annie who know how to make the best of them by saying conspiratorially, 'You have first pick and I'll have second.' I can see now that there was something childlike about her and that it gave her a kinship and sympathy with small children to which they quickly responded.

Afternoon excursions with Auntie Annie were unpredictable. Impossible to know whether at half-past four we should be climbing the hill to her house or entering Addison's, the confectioner's behind the pillars of a Victorian arcade in St. Leonards. It was then a very splendid place rich with gilt decoration and plush seats and in the window stood wonderful wedding-cakes or sugar tableaux made, Auntie Annie informed me, by Mr. Addison himself. To sit in Addison's opposite to Auntie Annie, who would say simple, adequate things like 'You may choose *two* cakes today,' seemed to me one of the happiest of my childhood's experiences. We would smile at one another and munch and not waste time on idle conversation.

She had other schemes for our mutual enjoyment. We might go all the way to Bexhill and back on the top of a tram, crossing the fields when the tramlines took a different way from the road. We might go on the pier and put three pennies in whichever machines we chose, so that their various merits had to be discussed carefully before we committed ourselves. Should it be the gipsy fortune-teller or the game of football?

Then again we might go up to Hastings Castle and see the dungeons, or into St. Clement's Caves, or out to Hollington to the church in the woods, or into Alexandra Park to see the reservoir. Or we might listen to the band, paying 2*d.* each for our deck-chairs. We would look at the bandsmen's brave uniforms or smile together at those people who got up and left their seats when they saw the ticket-collector coming.

Auntie Annie's home was a treasure-house of interesting things. It was Victorian Gothic in architecture and had the ugly exterior of its school, with hideous shrubs and an asphalt path in front of it and at the back a piece of lawn tended by a weekly jobbing gardener. Beyond this lawn was a stone memorial erected by Auntie Annie over the grave of her dog, Floss, inscribed with Floss's name, but it was not in the form of a cross, because that would not be right.

The interior of the house may well have been as ugly as the outside, but to me it was a place full of surprises, crowded with curious and delightful things, its drawers and cupboards stuffed with hoarded oddments from another age. The drawing-room, with windows tightly closed all the year round, had a smell of cedarwood and pot-pourri which Auntie Annie called 'Popery'.

'Why?' I asked.

'Because it's such a mixture,' she said.

In the drawing-room was a harmonium which Auntie Annie played on Sunday evenings when we came back from church, allowing me to choose my hymns from *Ancient and Modern*. But she also taught me to sing the *Ave Maria* from *Cavalleria Rusticana*, warning me to regard it as just a song and not think of it as having anything to do with religion. There was, too, a musical box of which the spring broke while I was playing it, scattering the blades of the metal comb with a frightening noise. It gives the measure of Auntie Annie's gentleness that instead of blaming me for this, as other grown-ups would, she giggled with me and put the fragments away without a word.

There was also, to be produced on special occasions, a stereoscope with a set of purplish photographs of Rome. Each had to be peered at in turn, and the eternal question 'How *does* it make things stand out like that?' puzzled Auntie Annie as much as it did me.

In all Auntie Annie's house there was scarcely any space not crowded with oddments. Mantelpieces, brackets, what-nots in every room held bewildering collections of china, silver, ornamental boxes, glass paperweights with flowers in them, ivory, fans, and ornate cases for every imaginable article—thimble-cases, scissors-cases, needle-cases. You picked up a little piece of ivory and found it had a peep-hole in it through which you discerned a magnified picture of the Eiffel Tower. You lifted the lid of a china orange and saw that it was full of old postage stamps. You opened a drawer and found a collection of old-fashioned games—halma, snakes-and-ladders, spillikins. The charms and wonders of that house, hidden or exposed, were inexhaustible.

There were books, but they were locked behind glass—not at all the sort of books that anyone thought of reading. Auntie Annie read the *St. Matthew's Parish Magazine* and tracts sent her by an organisation she supported for the conversion of Jews to Christianity, but not much else. When I was staying with her, anyhow, she and I had too much else to do, too many interesting things like playing hunt-the-slipper or cat's cradles or making a card castle.

But on Sunday a special atmosphere descended on the

house. It was not so much sterner, though some games were not allowed, but it was made different from other days in a hundred little ways. Prayers were longer, there was coffee instead of tea and Auntie Annie wore even more ornate clothes. At half-past ten, with the bells ringing of all the countless churches of Hastings and St. Leonards, we would set out for St. Matthew's, at which the service we attended was called on the notice-board 'Morning Prayer', as if in answer to the giddy and Romish term 'Mattins' used by other churches.

It is a red-brick church on a hill, and in those days, when the Vicar thundered from the pulpit for three-quarters of an hour every Sunday, it was filled almost to capacity. There was rustling and whispering before the Vicar entered, wearing the moustache which proclaimed that he had no affiliations with tonsures or the like, and the long white surplice and black stole which were as near to vestments as he allowed himself to go.

Auntie Annie, who wore her ermine coat to church in winter, looked solemn now. She would occasionally give me one of her little, kind smiles, but for the most part she was too awed by the Vicar to do anything but gaze up at him in the pulpit while he preached his long, polemical sermons. But the final hymn would come at last and we should find ourselves walking down the hill with the Misses Spiers, who shared Auntie Annie's prediliction for St. Matthew's. Then home to a huge lunch and a rest in the afternoon.

There was far too much food at Auntie Annie's, but then I was being 'built up' after an illness, so that is perhaps why her dining-table was so laden. Sometimes, too, she gave a dinner-party, and then there was no end to the little silver dishes of crystallised ginger, chocolates, almonds and raisins round the *epergne* in the centre of the table. The guests, of course, were the Misses Spiers, invariably and understandably called 'the Miss Spiers', and distinguished one from the other by being Miss Spiers and Miss Florence Spiers. I would be required to wear an Eton collar, and when we had gathered, the four of us, in the drawing-room, Auntie Annie would say, 'Now, Rupert, will you take Miss Spiers in to dinner?' So—at seven years old, perhaps—I would give the old lady my arm and we would march in pairs to the room next door.

Auntie Annie has been dead this quarter of a century or more and there is probably a garage where Floss's gravestone was, a television aerial over Emma's bedroom, sparse three-ply furniture in the rooms and prints of Van Gogh's noiser paintings on the walls. The crammed and miscellaneous contents of the house were dispersed by auction, I know, and Emma has a grown-up family of her own. I am glad that Auntie Annie did not, by too much, outlive her epoch or survive to be called a parasite and see her comfortable little income reduced to a pittance by taxation. ('Unearned income!' she used to say. 'It's *not* unearned. My father worked for every penny of it!') I am glad that she was never made to feel redundant, or to have her innocuous life called stagnant and useless, or to be shown the absurdity (and, of course, impossibility) of employing two servants to look after one single woman, to learn in fact that she had no right to exist at all. For all those things have happened to other Auntie Annies, and though no doubt the age is more advanced and efficient for their elimination, in goodness and gentleness it is poorer.

CHAPTER IX

Rose Hill

[1]

IT IS usual for the writer of today, remembering his or her youth, to express a good deal of self-pity. He was cruelly misunderstood, archaic kinds of education were inflicted on him, his parents were remote and he suffered from forced companionship. Most of us have known most of those things and the ideal upbringing has yet to be discovered, but there does not seem much point in moaning over all that and forgetting the compensations. Nor am I sure that the modern way of parents 'growing up again with their children', sympathising with their whims, having them psycho-analysed, coddling their smallest indispositions, encouraging their obstinacies and generally treating them as sacred beings will achieve so much better results.

Some of the things that the parents of those days did to their children were certainly tough, and I suspect that the apparent increase nowadays in cases of brutality comes from the greater efficiency of the societies combating it and from closer inspection of private life, rather than from any increase in the crime. 'Children should be seen and not heard' then, and were not encouraged to the detestable acts of exhibitionism of the modern child. I was kept in the nursery till I was old enough for a governess, and although my parents were kind and thoughtful I was rarely with them for long. 'Don't bother your father now; he's just come from London and he's tired,' my mother would say, though an hour or two earlier she would have told me that I must ask my father about that. There was no understanding of the terrible urgencies of childhood; there was no sympathy at all with a boy like me, who was 'never satisfied', 'always wanting something different'.

None of that mattered, I dare say, but at the age of just seven years I was sent as a boarder to a preparatory school, and that was rather brutal, though I was by no means the youngest child there. My parents came to my bedroom one night and said, 'You're going to boarding-school next week,' and left me to digest that. They had just returned, I found later, from a visit to Banstead across the downs, where they had been enchanted by the proprietors of Rose Hill School, Bertie Percy Browning and his wife. Term had started, the summer term of 1910, but Mrs. Browning in her rich, contralto voice had said that my mother was a friend of Alice Coubrough, a relative of hers, and that nothing should prevent her son being entered at once. So I was to be taken next week.

[2]

I have already in *Fall of Man* revealed some of the merits and evils of Rose Hill School and its staff—the Headmaster, known as Mr. B., a brown-skinned giant of great modesty and charm towards parents who used a cane with enthusiasm almost daily. Mrs. B., conspicuously dressed in the fashion of the day, *soignée* and deliciously scented, with a resonant and attractive speaking voice and a fine profile; a very siren, a Circe, with parents. I have mentioned some of the assistant masters and boys, but then had to turn to an imaginary incident to show its effect on the protagonist of my novel. I was not concerned with describing, bringing back into being, the school itself, because it was no more than a background for a part of my story.

What I find most disturbing when I remember my four years at Rose Hill School is that of all things I have recalled from before the First World War, a preparatory school is probably the least changed today. True, no longer on school walks do the leading boys intone 'Ca-a-a-r!' when a motor is in sight, a warning which used to be passed to those at the back. The masters no longer wear starched collars, and the school Sergeant has later decorations than those of the South African War. I suppose television has come to the classroom and there may be a small decline in the use of the cane. But otherwise what difference is there between the preparatory school of 1910 and its counterpart in 1958?

Certainly the curriculum has changed a mite, for the Common Entrance Examination makes slightly diffcrent demands from those who sit for it. But the same hidebound system, of allowing the entire mental training of boys in their most formative years to be limited and distorted by preparing them for one examination of narrow scope, still prevails, and as the financial success or failure of the preparatory school depends largely on the number of passes it achieves, its pupils have small chance of gaining any wider knowledge.

I wish the school I remember was as much a part of a vanished life as the home I have described. I wish its methods of teaching were outdated and the monstrous snobbishness of it a thing of the past. I wish I could be describing a quaint piece of Edwardian life which would have no place in the present. But I doubt it. I have an uncomfortable feeling that most of its characteristics persist in the preparatory schools of today.

The buildings it occupied are no longer used by a preparatory school, and Mr. and Mrs. B. died between the wars, but some of the assistant masters must surely be alive still and I have amused myself by finding the names of at least a dozen of my small contemporaries in the London Telephone Directory. That is how a freakish memory like mine plays tricks, for I can remember vividly and intimately a score or two of them as I knew them more than forty years ago, see their faces, hear their voices, recall their words and actions. The picture, as I write, is so strong that I can scarcely force myself to realise that those of them who have survived two world wars and all the other chances of life must be in their fifties now, with children and perhaps grandchildren of their own. It seems yesterday that I was talking with them, all of us in knickerbockers and Norfolk jackets, or on Sundays in Eton suits. It seems yesterday that I suffered the aching tedium and terror of the classrooms.

[3]

'Going back to school!'—the words still give me a ghostly disquiet. It was my first experience of doom; three days, two days, one day more of the holidays, then the grim, inevitable hour on which I would see the fly arrive like a hearse to carry me and my baggage away. Long free days in the garden and on the downs were over—for ever, as it seemed. Ninna must be kissed goodbye, the gardener, the dog, the pigeons, a heartbreaking series of adieux. No pleading would avail; nothing imaginable could postpone this harsh destiny by even an hour.

The long drive along the road towards the station, over the bridge and under the great beech trees, down to the lower road running under the downs then up the long slope of empty hillside to Banstead, I would have loved it all at any other time. I sat beside my mother instead of on the usual uncomfortable little seat with its back to the driver, because today there were only two of us.

Then we arrived at the big Georgian house with its

additional modern wings. It had once been a private mansion and the dining-room had been a picture gallery and ballroom. Even as a school it kept its dignity and the door was opened by a footman in full regalia and we were shown to the large drawing-room where Mrs. B. would be at her most opulently charming and Mr. B. at his most retiring. Tea would be brought in—I have the impression of almost too much silver and of the tiniest cakes—and other parents with their boys would be cleverly introduced till the large room was full of chattering ladies with their offspring.

At last would come the cruel moment of execution— 'Time for your mother to go now'—and the leading away into captivity. My stomach sinks and turns now as I remember it.

It was not that it was a particularly hard school by contemporary standards or that there was bullying in it, or that we were underfed or treated badly. On the contrary, except for Mr. B.'s too ready cane, there was nothing to fear. The food was good, the dormitories scrupulously clean, the school Matron a qualified nurse and the assistant masters the best that could be obtained. The grounds and gardens were larger than necessary and extremely well kept, the school had its own dairy produce and vegetables and its boys were coached by first-rate cricketers and footballers. On the face of it, it was excellent, and even today I am convinced that it was far better than most schools of its kind at the time or of the present. Yet not one of us, as we left our parents in the hall and were led, suppressing tears, to the big schoolroom where all were assembling, felt anything but a sick sense of despair. It was school as opposed to home, discipline instead of indulgence, lessons instead of wanderings and adventures, and always, the sword of Damocles, Mr. B.'s cane. It was not a very good life for a small boy.

L

[4]

So at seven I was thrown into this, and soon aped the other children in following the routine. The smallest of us slept in a room with eight beds under the immediate and baleful eye of Matron and the direct care of Mrs. B.

Matron was never seen except in the dress and trappings of a hospital nurse, a heavy, humourless woman skilled in distinguishing between real and imaginary ailments and quick to follow Mrs. B.'s lead in knowing which boys to make a fuss over. These, I fear, were the sons of the richer or more famous parents, certainly not children like me, who were admitted on slightly reduced terms. But to be fair, all of us were looked after well by Mrs. B. and Matron and their favouritism was not blatant.

Each in turn would come into the 'little boys' dormitory' to say good night, Mrs. B. with a rustle of silk before she went down to the staff dinner, a rather grand nightly occasion. I can still hear her resonant 'Good night, boys!' and catch the ghost of her discreet perfume.

I remember the occupants of all eight beds. There was Cedric Keith-Jones, who, we knew, was the son of one of the partners in Keith Prowse and Company, even then well-known, though long before they had adopted the phrase by which they were later famous—'You want the best seats. We have them.' There was a boy called Hennessy whose father was connected with the great brandy firm and another called Nutt, the son of the proprietor of the Sea View Hotel at Ryde. Archie Ghosal, the only Indian in the school, was related to the Maharajah of Cooch Behar and had the most wonderful parents, who would come down with princely gifts for the whole school so that we would be eating sweets for days after their visits. Archie once had a basket of mangoes sent him and gave me one—the most deliciously exotic thing I had tasted.

Then Eddie Campbell Cooper, a solicitor's son who came from Chipstead; and Watts, who was American; and Nash, who was an actor's son and had a photo of his late father, a fine-looking man, beside his bed. It will be noticed that even now I remember their fathers' professions, for these were the days when new boys in schools like this were asked, 'What's your name?' and 'What's your father?'

The smallest of us had learnt to dress himself and run down to the big schoolroom where the forty or fifty boys gathered. If I saw it now, I suppose, I should find a large room, thirty feet long perhaps, but from childhood one remembers everything on a vast scale and the schoolroom seems enormous. Chatter, chatter, 'You're a beast,' 'Matron's a fool,' 'Have you heard about Strickland?' 'Bet Mr. B. gives it hot to Sanderson,' until a large handbell rung by Moss the footman told us that it was time to get into pairs to march through to breakfast.

Through three classrooms we went, across the entrance hall of the private part of the house, then into a dark passage in the servants' quarters, to emerge in the dining-room itself. This again seems vast, and in fact was a large, very high room in which a dozen tables, each for six boys and a master, could be set at some distance from one another, while a high table, at which sat Mr. and Mrs. B. in state, was twelve feet from the nearest.

Before breakfast were some rather perfunctory prayers read by Mr. B. from beside a harmonium at the far end of the room, preceded by four verses of a hymn. Mrs. B. would play the harmonium for these, making her entry when the boys had gathered. She used to wear the blouse and skirt of the time with usually a little velvet bow-tie clasped at the neck with a small diamond brooch. She would greet us in her rich voice as she approached and we would pipe a reply in chorus.

Those hymns! *Through the Night of Doubt and Sorrow* we

would carol merrily, or *Oft in Danger, Oft in Woe*, or *New Every Morning is the Love*. We knew the words by heart, for there was a choice of only about eight, and Mrs. B. would say which one it was to be.

Then to breakfast—sausages one day, kedgeree, bacon and fried bread, scrambled eggs, smoked haddock, brawn on others, and always on Saturdays new rolls, butter and treacle. But these were preceded every morning with good porridge, sugar and milk. Mrs. B. was not a parsimonious caterer.

I remember breakfast chiefly, though, as the time when we would observe and discuss those high Olympians, the assistant masters, as each came in and took his place. There was Mr. Parker, known as Posh, the senior assistant, a rolling, stout man with greying hair and moustache who gave little scope for hero-worship, as he taught mathematics with deadly persistency and a good deal of recourse to Mr. B.'s cane, always readily used on receipt of a note from an assistant master. He was, I believe, a good coach both in mathematics and football, but he was not elegant, dashing or popular, so we had to be content with rather meaningless recrimination.

Next in seniority was Mr. Berkeley. R.M.B.—I can see his initials still on one of the notes to Mr. B. which were death sentences in themselves. He was tall and rather handsome in spite of protruding ears, his hair was long and wavy, he wore nice easy clothes and he was a good all-round athlete. There were those, in fact, who maintained that Mr. Berkeley was the most popular master in the school, and it could be seen that he was at least popular with Mr. and Mrs. B., for it was his daily custom to leave his place towards the end of breakfast and stand at the high table chatting comfortably with them. 'Bet Mr. and Mrs. B. like Mr. Berkeley terrifically' might be heard among us.

There was always a French master, at first little old M.

Godard, who had been at the school for ages, but was never popular with Mrs. B. 'Bet Mrs. B. *hates* Monsieur Godard,' we said, no doubt with exaggeration. After I had been at Rose Hill School for a few terms, he was replaced by dear M. Gazère, a tall Provençal with untidy hair and a brown moustache, who was the only master beside whom I used to keep when we took a school walk. This was not difficult, as it would have been with more spectacular and popular masters. Their 'sides' would be 'bagged' three deep. 'Bags I next to Mr. Berkeley.' 'I've bagged it.' 'Bags I his other side.' 'Fowler's bagged that.' 'Bags I next to you, then.' And so on. But with M. Gazère I could walk and, incredible eccentricity, try to talk French. Moreover, I used to write letters to him in French in the holidays.

Then there was Mr. Allen, 'A.W.A.' on notes to Mr. B. 'Mr. Allen's easily the brainiest master in the school.' 'Mr. Allen's terrifically brainy.' I truly believe he was. He used to give lectures instead of prep. once or twice a term on subjects as varied as the life of the bee and Inca civilisation. He was a bald young man of great physical strength who wore rimless pince-nez and rather nondescript clothes. A ready note-sender, he was a successful inculcator of facts. He was considered 'strict'. 'Mr. Allen's beastly strict.' But one thing endeared him to us all. When he played cricket, as he did on the yearly occasion of Fathers' Match, he batted briefly, but two or three balls in every over he hit for six. We sat round the field in delight and wonder and made a noise like a high-piping siren as each went over the trees. It was, of course, what every one of us was longing to be able to do as we wearily learnt strokes at the nets, and it sent inhibitions flying all round the field. 'Mr. Allen's a ripping slogger,' we told new boys who had not seen the performance.

Last came those two dashing young men, the *beaux ideals* of preparatory scholarship, the heroes and idols of the

school, Mr. Townsend and Mr. Alford. Mr. Townsend was
a little older, taller and leaner than Mr. Alford, a conventionally handsome young man who spent—one cannot help
feeling even at this distance—too much money on clothes.
Mr. Alford had just left Clifton and, as I see now, was a
pleasant enough youth with too much dark, straight hair
smarmed down with brilliantine. They divided the school
into two well-balanced sides. 'Mr. Townsend's easily the
best-dressed master in the school,' 'Bet he's not. Bet Mr.
Alford's better dressed,' and so on. The battle raged for
years until, shortly before the outbreak of war, Mr. Townsend left with the romantic intention of going into the motor
business. It was a severe blow to the partisans of Mr. Alford,
when, during the following term, Mr. Townsend arrived
in a brilliant scarlet motor car. But Mr. Alford recouped
somewhat when, on the outbreak of war, he volunteered to
join the Army, and on leaving at the end of the term was
presented by the school with a new shining sword.

So they came to breakfast, the assistant masters, and did
not encourage the boys at their tables to talk too much, but
gave hints sometimes of their heroic life outside the school,
of a visit to the moving pictures or a drive to Sutton. We
goggled at them, at seven and eight years old, and were told
by Matron to eat our breakfasts.

Then we 'walked round' for half an hour or so. There
was almost an acre of lawn behind the house with a paved
path about it and we wandered chattering round this. This
was invariable in fine weather unless it was the birthday of
Mr. B. or one of the other masters, when there was a quaint
ceremony in the big schoolroom, for we would have subscribed for a present, which was handed over the desk to its
bashful recipient amid applause and a half-holiday promised
in return. That, perhaps, was more of its period than most
things I am describing; the tall desk, the thirteen-year-old
Head Boy on one side of it, forty or fifty boys crowding

round him, clambering over the desks (for it was an occasion of privilege and ordinary rules were forgotten), then the master who had to be summoned as though he did not know what was taking place, receiving his packet, opening it and expressing delight at his silver match-box or new walking-stick. Or could it all happen today?

Lessons began at nine o'clock. We faced hours of a hateful, unrelieved mixture of boredom and fear. We approached no subject with any real interest and certainly none with enthusiasm. 'How weary, stale, flat and unprofitable' it all was. Latin in dreary chants—*amo, amas, amat; mensa, mensa, mensam.* History in another meaningless sing-song rhythm—*William the First Ten Sixty-Six; William the Second Ten Eighty-Seven.* Geography in the same manner—Northumberland, Cumberland, Durham. Geometry with theorems learnt by heart, theorems which could have been understood in ordinary language but which, read out in all the nonsensical set phraseology of our geometry books, were incomprehensible to me, at least. French in the same runic way. I remember chanting *doodeladay, du, de la, des,* again and again till thirty times were counted without in the least knowing what the rather pretty combination of syllables signified.

Worst of all was English, a subject which at that time came low in importance in the scale of things learnt for Common Entrance. English had two branches, Dictation and Rep. Dictation was intended to teach us the use of our language, its spelling and punctuation. From Dictation we learnt all we were destined to learn of the subtleties, the delights, the infinite pliability, the rich vocabulary, the economy and the grace of the most versatile of the world's languages. From Rep., or learning by heart and expressionlessly repeating passages of Kipling's or Newbold's poetry, we were to form the basis of a love and knowledge of the greatest literature of the Christian era. At thirteen we should be able to pass the Common Entrance Examination, even perhaps obtain a scholarship at, one of the public schools. But at the age when Alexander was being tutored by Aristotle, Chatterton writing fifteenth-century verse, and any French boy with his first amorous experiences behind him reading his own classics for pleasure, we had no knowledge of the world's formation or development, none of its ancient or modern history. Few names of men and women in the long string stretching from ancient Egypt to modern America were even known to us, and, asked who Plato, Charlemagne, Richelieu or Lincoln were, we should have gaped. We were blankly ignorant of the most elementary facts of biology, zoology, indeed of any ology or subject other than the desiccated scraps of knowledge considered necessary for the passing of an examination. We had been caned and cajoled into the possession of a number of disconnected and mostly insignificant facts, foreign words and figures, and that was all. Worst of all, nothing that we had learnt in class had for a moment interested us.

Still, we trooped into our airy, well-lighted little classrooms every morning and sat at desks round Mr. Berkeley or Mr. Allen and the drill of lessons began. By eleven o'clock, our fingers inky from the pots into which we dipped wooden pens, our brains confused with active and passive tenses, the houses of York and Lancaster, lines of latitude and longitude, *avoir* and *être*, and all the rest of the hotch-potch we were supposed to retain, we went out for the break. A walk through the big kitchen gardens, along cinder-paths between high box edges, took us chattering to the playing-fields for a kick-about in winter or scrappy moments of cricket in summer. By a different route strolled the assistant masters in their tweed caps, smoking their manly pipes.

After another hour's work came a short interval before lunch. If during the morning one had received a note for Mr. B., this was the time to present it. 'Has done no work at all this morning. A.W.A.' 'Will not try. R.M.B.' Any such phrase in the neat handwriting of one of the assistant masters was sufficient, for Mr. B. was not particular about the phraseology.

His study occupied a strategic position between the private part of the house and the schoolrooms and had a door leading into each. With manfully suppressed tears one knocked and, if there was no reply, one entered and stood just inside the door waiting for Mr. B. to arrive. One had not much heart to look about the room, at the thick-piled carpet and comfortable armchairs, at the engraved silver or the well-framed sporting prints, or even at the inscribed oar on the wall. Soon Mr. B., with the swinging walk of a tall man, would come down the hall and take the note from one's hand.

He did not waste much time on idle chatter.

'Why have you done no work this morning?' he might ask, or 'What do you mean by refusing to try?'

One made one's tearful defence, but might just as well have remained silent, for Mr. B. was busy selecting a cane and did not seem to hear. Then the terrifying cuts, far too heavily given, even for a much older boy, and to the small ones that we were nothing short of brutal.

Perhaps it did us no harm. Perhaps Mr. B. knew no other way to get us through the Common Entrance Examination. Perhaps he even disliked this daily thrashing of children. I certainly bear him no grudge, nor any to the young men who wrote those notes. It was the acknowledged system of the day, and it would have been an eccentric preparatory school proprietor who never used a cane—one who might soon be given the dangerous reputation of being crankish. Whether it left any evil effects on natures more sensitive than mine is another matter. According to psychiatrists, no doubt, we shall bear the scars in our subconscious minds to the end of our lives. Whatever the truth, I remember it only as a hateful and frightening thing which was a perpetual threat during my four years at Rose Hill School, the thing which made the sharpest distinction between the bliss of home and the purgatory of school.

[5]

Lunch was a pleasant meal because the terrors of Mr. B.'s study were relieved for the time being. When it was over, but while we still sat at table, Matron would rise slowly to her feet, cross the room, and, with nearly all eyes on her, solemnly unlock the Tuck Cupboard. This was the big moment of the day for Matron and for the luckier boys, too, for she would portion out the sweets which their parents had sent them, allowing four toffees here, three chocolate biscuits there, until enough had been distributed, and the cupboard was locked again.

Now was the time to observe whatever craze was rampant, for we had half an hour or more of idleness in the big schoolroom. There was always some craze and there were always boys who showed the greatest ingenuity in it. Once, for instance, it was the thing to cut out the shape of an aeroplane from paper, fold it neatly so that the wings were exactly balanced, weight the nose with a nib and throw it dart-like. A boy called Lawson, the son of a famous Brighton jeweller, became so adept that he produced a biplane which, released from the gallery at one end of the big schoolroom, hit the wall at almost the same height at the other end. At another time the craze was miniature cardboard theatres, which were mounted and lit by the bulb from a torch. This must have been a craze in other schools too, for sets of scenery and cut-out characters were sold for many famous plays, and I remember watching a much-abbreviated version—it took ten minutes—of *The Corsican Brothers*. This was produced by a clever boy called York

Miller, whose mother, Elizabeth York Miller, was a famous novelist at that time and nearly always had a serial running in one of the daily papers.

There were those of us who, having our own private interests, remained apart from crazes. Frank Vosper, for instance, took no part in the craze for toy theatres, but spent his time in drawing. He was, incidentally, the only boy of this school I knew in after-life, and his tragic and mysterious death twenty years later was a private loss as well as a general one. A big red-headed boy called Foster-Brown had his own steam engine which puffed and rattled near the toy cupboard, until one day the methylated spirit spilled and became ignited and the steam engine had to be confiscated.

In summer we had afternoon lessons, then went to play cricket; in winter we played football first, then came in to the classrooms. How splendid were the assistant masters in their blazers! What heroes as they casually came on to the field, abandoning their pipes, to bowl at the nets for a while or to umpire. But here again the system was against all but the aptest of the boys. Matches had to be won against other preparatory schools, for, as every proprietor knew, a reputation as a good cricket or football school meant swelling numbers and profits. So members of the school team and juniors who shaped well for it were coached assiduously, and boys of no particular ability or promise were neglected.

How well I remember coming back from the cricket field for tea, tired, yet somehow exalted by the hour or two of sunlight and the game, chattering with one of a dozen boys of my own age. The smell of the vegetable garden and the herb garden nearer the house is in my nostrils now. A hurried wash, a secret swallowing of a little tap water to ease the hot thirst (strictly forbidden, that), then in to tea to see whose jam or cake was on the table. Perhaps it was

mine, so that I would have the great privilege of offering
it to the boys at my table and Matron, then taking it to offer
to Mr. Townsend, perhaps, or Mr. Alford, whichever was
momentarily enshrined.

After tea there was nearly an hour, I think, of blissful
playing with other excited sunburnt small boys before we
were summoned to prep.

I can remember so many of those boys that I shall appear
to be boasting of a phenomenal memory if I mention more
than a few, and those because they seem typical of the time
and the school. Great names of commerce were common
among us. There was Russell Dickins, whose father was a
partner in Dickins and Jones; and a charming slim boy, a
good athlete called Hamley, son of the famous toy-maker,
and a very tall popular boy, John Sich, whose name was
on many public-house signs in those days, for before the
great combines had swallowed up all the family breweries
Sich's Ales were well-known. With the small blond person
of Graham Murdoch were associated three more great
commercial names, for his father was the managing director
of the piano firm, one of his uncles was A. W. Gamage and
another the proprietor of the then universally advertised
Skuse's Sweets. There was a quiet boy called Rickett whose
father's firm of coal merchants was then well known as
Rickett, Smith and Company, and Bourchier, who was a
son or nephew of Arthur Bourchier, whose name we all
knew as an actor, and a cheerful little Welsh boy called
Davies whose uncle was Lloyd George. They crowd back
to memory; Pugh, who came from Exeter and used to
lend me his watch sometimes (a large silver affair, for no
one had a wrist-watch then); Tracy Holmes, whose father
had driven at Brooklands at sixty miles an hour; the
Schulman brothers from Brazil and the Bearman brothers,
the school's most popular athletes; the Alloms, sons of a
famous engineer, who was in some way connected with

Mrs. B., and Adair Coubrough, whose mother and mine had been friends as girls. Then Peter Downes, who broke my tooth with a cricket ball; Roberts, the son of a Croydon Vicar who had a pleasing trick of imitating a monkey, and a very handsome boy called Grunwald, whose name was changed to Greenhill on the outbreak of war and who, to the grief of the school, died during the second term of wartime.

This is absurd. I am sitting in a Tangier villa without any printed matter from that time, and I find that I can name and remember almost every one of those little boys who raced through the corridors of Rose Hill School more than forty years ago. Evers, who afterwards became a Wimbledon tennis-player; Cuff, who won the Victor Ludorum Cup; the Davies brothers, the Miller twins, Nothmann from Brazil, Field, Pepper; Metcalf, whose father was a horse-trainer; Colam and Burnside, whom I met later at Tonbridge; an Admiral's son named Robinson; Malone, Norris, Lewin, Hay; Warden, with whom I had a fight; the Tilden brothers, one of whom upset a cup of tea over my mother's dress on Sports Day; Baddeley, Bateson, Mackenzie, Perreira; Fowler, who was Mr. Berkeley's nephew; Jerome, whose father was on the Stock Exchange. This is becoming tiresome and must stop.

But you will see that we were the sons of prosperous middle-class parents, and will guess that we looked and were very much like the boys of a good preparatory school today.

[6]

There were two visiting instructors, Mr. Gisby and the Sergeant. Mr. Gisby gave piano lessons to those who 'took' music as an 'extra' and taught singing to the whole school. Mr. Gisby had plump, pasty cheeks, soft, soulful eyes and a moustache with little waxed points. His hair was long, dark and loose. It was parted in the middle and scattered dandruff over the collar of his suit. He wore, moreover, a very high starched collar without a fold in it, like a cuff, round his neck and bound it with a tie or stock in which there was a large pearl pin. So much of Mr. Gisby's habitual wear has disappeared that I do not even know the name for it. What, for instance, did they call those white linings protruding at the V of a waistcoat? Mr. Gisby was never without one or without his large looped watch-chain. His get-up was designed to show that he was a being apart, an artist, a musician.

Do such instructors still live by teaching for a day a week in each of several schools, like jobbing gardeners? If so, I cannot believe that they dress and act the part with the sentimental *abandon* of Mr. Gisby, who almost wept at the false notes in our part-songs, and stamped his foot and waved his arms as though he were impersonating a temperamental foreign conductor.

What guided Mr. Gisby in his choice of songs for us I cannot imagine, for I remember our singing, in English, of course, the Bridal March from *Lohengrin*:

'Faithful and true we lead ye forth
Where love triumphant shall crown ye with joy,
Star of renown, Flower of the earth,
Blest be ye both far from all life's alloy.'

So we piped, not very appropriately one would have thought, while Mr. Gisby gesticulated and tore his hair and banged down the lid of the piano in despair.

Our other visiting instructor, the Sergeant, was temperamentally Mr. Gisby's opposite, but he, too, in make-up and manner knew his part. He had a rather sour, old soldier's face and looked as though he did not think his pension was enough to compensate him for thirty years of soldiering, in which he was probably justified. He shouted at us, by an effort modulating the parade-ground manner with which he had made recruits tremble, doubtless, from Calcutta to Cape Town.

He came on Mondays, and instead of going into class we would put on gym-shoes and line up in the gymnasium. Drill would be followed by exercises, and that hour a week was the only time we gave to all that is now called P.T., or to military training, which occupy so much of the modern boy's day. I am glad to remember that I was hopelessly bad at drill then as for the rest of my life. I was a butt for the Sergeant's rallies and could never manage to keep in step.

Whatever may have happened to visiting music masters, the jobbing sergeant must certainly be a thing of the past, for surely the modern counterpart of any of our assistant masters could teach us all the Sergeant did of drill and P.T. without any increase in the salary already paid him 'with board and residence'. But before the First World War a preparatory school sergeant was an ornament which no proprietor could afford to be without, for his Zulu and Boer War ribbons looked well and his usefulness could be expounded in the prospectus. ('A qualified school sergeant', whatever that may mean.)

[7]

The wild happiness that came at the end of term almost compensated for the hours of fear and boredom. Breaking-up day seen from a week before was scarcely credible, scarcely even imaginable; its promise was too glorious. At nine years old I half awoke at night to find myself doing imaginary Latin exercises on the pillow, so drilling and relentless were methods of teaching in a school like that. Those 'lessons', which one can now see as idiotically mis-directed and crushing, suddenly ended in sublime relief.

Small boys' brains are ready enough to be filled, but not
by dull, irrelevant and disconnected facts like the capital of
Portugal is Lisbon, the plural of *je suis* is *nous sommes*. All the
hours of having these facts drilled into us, all the weeks of
daily lessons, became, in one radiant day, things of the past,
unreal, totally unimportant.

On the incredible morning of Breaking-up a horse-
drawn char-à-banc would take most of the boys to Sutton
Station, from which they would go to London. But Eddie
Campbell Cooper and I would wait until they had left, then
walk across the downs to Chipstead. He was considered a
rather wild and unpredictable boy, one of only three in
the school, incidentally, who wore glasses, for the oculists
had not yet frightened us all into submission.

Children, I think, have more capacity for deep and
powerful emotion than we imagine or remember. The love
of a child can be heartbreaking and his tragedies and
triumphs overpowering. From our own experience of the
stress of grown-up emotions we are apt to belittle the
potency of childhood's, and few of us realise what home-
coming can mean in ecstasy to a small boy or girl. To arrive
at Wayside from Rose Hill School at the end of term was
for me happiness beyond reality. I probably expressed it by
behaving in a way that would be called silly or by showing
off; I certainly could not put it into words, even had I
wanted to. But I know now that the overwhelming bliss I
felt comes rarely in childhood and with such completeness
never in later life.

CHAPTER X

Changes and Chances

[1]

THE FIRST of my grandparents to die was my Grandmother Cooke, and I remember it only as an occasion on which I was told not to worry my father because he was very upset.

Soon afterwards my uncle Edward Taylor arrived at Wayside in his Sunbeam motor car to take my father and mother over to see my Grandmother Taylor, who was very ill, and at the last minute I was made one of the party. I remember seeing the little Kingston house for the last time, a hush among its knick-kacks and fripperies. I was taken upstairs to my grandmother's room to kiss someone shrivelled and frail and feeble-voiced lying among lace and linen. I was told a few days later rather morbidly that I had been the only one of my generation to see my grandmother in the week before she died.

The last to go was 'the Emperor', and that only after a long, fighting illness with a trained nurse as ally in his struggle to survive. His death was the first that had any real meaning for me, the first that gave me any sense of loss.

It was followed by a crisis of a kind known in most families like mine, in which long and involved wills and bequests mean lasting antagonisms and often costly litigation among those who remain. 'The Emperor', it appeared, at some time during the vacillating fortunes of my father's early married life, had advanced him a sum of money which had remained invested for the old man. During the last

M

months of his life he had added a codicil cutting out my father since, as the codicil explained, he would benefit by this sum, a far lesser one than his share of the estate. My father was convinced that this had been done at the instigation of his brothers, and it was from then that my uncle, Herbert Cooke, became 'that scoundrel' and my Uncle Selwyn 'a poor weak fool under his influence'.

It was not, I think, the actual loss which distressed my father, for 'the Emperor' had not left a fortune, but the manifest unfairness of the thing and the feeling that his father had acted secretively against him. He was convinced, and I am sure rightly, that only during his last illness and under pressure would 'the Emperor' have acted as he did.

I was quite unaware of the details at the time, but there were some dark weeks at my home only slightly relieved when my father went down to my uncle's parish of Belbroughton and insisted on a settlement which, though not a satisfactory one, he eventually obtained.

Is there a middle-class English family without some such story as this? Victorian will-making bred every kind of disaccord and few of the later generations escape their consequences. I was faced with an almost identical situation forty years later and know the sense of betrayal and the pain which my father felt then.

[2]

A greater loss to me was announced in a letter from my mother while I was at school. Ninna was leaving us and going to Canada.

This was a blow from which I have never, in a sense, recovered. It meant that no trust could be put in destiny, in human nature, in the permanence of things as I knew them. Ninna had been more surely a part of life even than my parents; she was arbiter and guide, she was *there* as much as home and family were there. Yet when I returned to Wayside she would be gone, and I should never see her again. It was a blow against security and faith as well as an acute personal loss. I cried several nights secretly under the bedclothes in the 'little boys' dormitory' at school. I had been long enough there to know that it would be suicide to confide in anyone. A nurse of any kind was not to be mentioned among the tough young men we had now become; to admit fondness for one and distress at her departure would be like admitting that you missed your mummy.

I did miss Ninna dreadfully and, since, of course, none of us grows up in anything less superficial than grey hair and false teeth, I have missed her ever since. Who does not, at eight or eighty, miss someone to go to in trouble, someone who is never at a loss, someone who feels with one both triumph and disaster, someone who always understands?

To Canada. I hated the very name of the place for years.

[3]

But the other people about me remained and if they changed I did not perceive it.

My Aunt Fo-Fo had taken her basket-work and net-making outfit, her paint-box and potter's clay and gone to live with the Edward Taylors at Woldingham in an attractive house with a terraced garden. The hearty Taylor uncles appeared from time to time with their wives, from India or South Africa or, the engineer, from the North of England. Neither of those on leave from abroad brought any of the magic of far places with them, either in concrete or abstract form, and it strikes me now that they must have been unimaginative men not to realise what some trivial piece of tourist's goods would have meant to a stay-at-home family like ours, and more unimaginative still to have been unable to say anything suggesting to eager-minded children the exotic marvels in their lives.

I do remember once asking my uncle Herbert Taylor, the army doctor, what it was like in Singapore.

'Hot,' he replied with undeniable truth. I could well sympathise with this if it had been intended as a snub to a tiresomely inquisitive child, but it was nothing of the sort. It was all he had noticed about the place. Or all he could communicate.

One of the Cooke aunts, Eirene, had been loyal to my father in the family rift, and she used to come and stay with us for several weeks in every year after 'the Emperor's' death. With her grey clothes and knitted woollen shawl, she would sit in the garden at Wayside, always insisting on doing something useful, shelling peas or darning stockings. Then out would come an example of the esoteric vocabulary evolved by those brothers and sisters in the days of 'the Emperor's' tyranny, pieces of foreign language learnt from him or the curious misuse of English words to which they gave a new significance. My father's family continued to use them till the end of their lives.

A wasp would annoy my aunt Eirene.

'*Allez-vous en*,' she would say as she waved it away. I learned the little phrase at once and used it ten years later, with disastrous results, on a French lady-of-the-town who approached me in the promenade during the interval at the Folies Bergère.

'That's all luscious,' would say my aunt Eirene or my father, meaning 'That's all right', or 'That's all glory', with the same significance.

There were some odd redundancies in their diction; things were not merely dirty, they were 'filthy-dirty'; people not just base, but 'the lowest of the low'. My aunt and father used current terms of comparison, 'thick as thieves' and 'good as gold', and some rather exaggerated language in abuse or praise of others who might be 'vile beasts' or 'sweetly pretty'.

When my Aunt Eirene came to stay with us at the seaside she would go down to a shelter on the front and sit doing crochet work until someone took a seat near her, preferably a woman of her own age, whom my aunt would ensnare into conversation. By polite cross-examination, which would have done credit to a skilled lawyer, in ten minutes my aunt would have elicited the most intimate facts of her new friend's life and family and, according to my father, revealed her own. As one approached the shelter, one would see my aunt with her feet up on the seat ('Awful common thing to do,' my father said), busy with her crochet and looking up from it to smile at someone she had known for barely half an hour.

'And is your daughter married?' one might hear, or 'Where does your sister live now?'

It was nearly always obvious that her new acquaintance was enjoying the conversation as much as my aunt. They had become 'thick as thieves'.

My Aunt Xenia, on the other hand, while not entirely siding with 'that scoundrel', had not given my father all the loyalty he felt entitled to expect and for a short time suffered interdiction. But that must have passed, since I remember visiting her ugly home at Norwood with my father. It was not a happy occasion, but it had one interesting moment when on the way back we saw from the top of a tram a kindly-looking old gentleman walking in the grounds of a large house.

'That,' said my father, 'is Jabez Balfour, the Liberator Bond swindler. He has been in prison for years.'

Others who reappeared at intervals during those years when I was at Rose Hill were the Walter Smiths, who always came like the three kings bearing gifts. Annie Dickson came, too, but I remember little of her visits, seeing her only in her house at St. Leonards-on-Sea. But once when I had been home for a day's holiday at half-term and so hated the thought of return to Rose Hill and lessons and Mr. B.'s study that I cried desperately at the breakfast table, I remember her doing the only thing she could think of—handing me half a crown.

[4]

An institution of the time which survives only in an emasculated form was that of godparents. Every child in families like mine had at least two of these, carefully chosen, not for the moral qualities or the sense of responsibility required, one would have supposed, in those who 'promise for me in my Baptism', but for their wealth, generosity or heirlessness.

Godparents in those days knew their duties. They did not necessarily attend the child's christening, but they never failed to send a thing called a 'christening mug', a useless piece of embossed silver holding less than half a pint, and thereafter remembering their godchild on his birthdays, at Christmas and in their wills. It was a harmless way of securing a little mild patronage for children, though it is hard to see what religious significance attached to it.

By the only standards thought important, I was lucky in mine. My godfather was Philip Croft, the only son of my Great-uncle Septimus. I did not see him more than once, on the platform of a London station, and he lives in my mind only as a splendid man with a white silk scarf. But the presents he sent me were the most lavish that came to our home, a magnificent model yacht, a large clockwork gunboat which crossed ponds under its own power and later a clay pigeon shooting outfit.

My godmother seemed to me then a remote, beautiful and gracious person. She was an old friend of my mother's called Bella Whitehead, a maiden lady sharing a pleasant Hampstead flat with her sister. Later I came to know and admire her, but in childhood she seemed a very angel, descending on our home occasionally and appearing at dinner dressed—or must I be mistaken?—in cream satin. For fifty years until her death a few years ago she never forgot a single birthday or Christmas, and her little packets have reached me in strange corners of the world. Then she was to me an occasional presence, elegant, fragrant, and adorable, not yet a person.

[5]

We were never in that state spoken of with commiseration and solemnity as 'without servants', though it cost my mother many days of wearisome search to be able to replace the women who worked for a time and left. Domestic service as it had been throughout the previous eighty years was already on the wane. We had always a cook and housemaid, but none stayed with us for more than a year or two, for the days were over when both employer and servant accepted one another with their faults for the remainder of life.

Housemaids wore uniform then—large aprons and caps over plain blue dresses in the morning, neat lace aprons and caps over black dresses in the afternoon. They rose at six and the house was clean before we came down to breakfast already laid in the dining-room by a brightly burning fire. They laid and cleared away three meals a day and had duties referred to in set phrases—doing the stairs, making the beds, waiting at table, drawing the blinds, opening the front door (this included taking cards on a silver tray), turning down the beds. They had one 'afternoon out' a week and earned £2 a month.

There were still women who accepted this life—for that matter, there were still plenty who chose and liked it, for it relieved all anxiety about ways and means of keeping alive which had probably troubled them since childhood. But there were not enough to make the employer's position an easy one. I remember visits to Purley with my mother, to some stuffy room of a small house called a Registry Office, where an ageing and unhealthy-looking woman grudgingly handed over a couple of addresses in return for a 'registration fee'. Then we would tramp to the address and my mother would interview the prospective cook or housemaid.

'What experience have you? Have you a reference from your last place? Are you married or single?' And so on. It was noteworthy that in return the housemaid asked my mother nothing, for it would have been impertinent of a servant to ask the most elementary question about her future circumstances.

There was still something to be said for domestic service; it still had shreds of dignity and orderliness about it. In later years, between the wars, it grew anachronistic and absurd, and middle-class ladies were reduced to the humiliation of persuading some ham-fisted slut to dress up as a housemaid for the sake of appearances. The disappearance now of that mockery can scarcely be regretted by anyone, least of all by the housewife, but the servants of my childhood were women who knew their work and found no anomaly in it.

They came and went. There was an old cook called Thyer of vicious temper and superlative ability. ('We must never lose this woman, Lucy.') There was an unpleasant housemaid who left to get married after two months and wrote a rude letter to my parents while she was on her honeymoon. There was a large, laconic woman with a goitre whose cooking was excellent, though she would 'never do enough vegetables', a cardinal sin in my father's eyes. There were Marys and Marthas and other women with names considered suitable for domestic service, for if they were called anything less humdrum, like Cynthia or Olivia, simpler names were immediately found for them. Two syllables were considered quite enough for any house-maid's name.

They learned their duties, if they did not already know them, referred to my father and mother as 'the master' and 'the mistress', stayed for a few months or a few years and left, usually after scrupulously giving the correct period of notice. Some of them were even dismissed. One asthmatic housemaid who wheezed when she handed the dishes had to be given notice for breathing.

On the whole they were happy enough and took their work and circumstances as a matter of course. It was not only the difficulty of replacing them which made my parents what was called 'considerate with the servants', and for me as a child this led to the severest form of discipline I knew. 'Don't do that; it will upset the servants.' 'Don't make a lot of extra washing-up for them to do.' Such prohibitions were natural enough then, but in later years one heard them in every household spoken with anxiety, almost with terror.

[6]

There was no gramophone in my home, for my father was quite without interest in music and my mother had her piano. She was a fine pianist who could, and perhaps should, have been a professional. No doubt she would have been better employed in making music than in bringing into the world my brothers, my sister and myself.

Her favourite composers were Beethoven, Chopin and Mendelssohn, with Schumann and Schubert a long way behind and a few small fry, including the tinkling Madame Chaminade, for lighter moments. Perhaps she had no great taste in music, but that is lacking in many good performers. She had competence, versatility and feeling.

Before the piano was a square seat with a front which swung open a little way to reveal racks of music and was apt to slam dangerously on one's fingers, but the bound volumes of Beethoven, red cloth with gilt *Sonaten* on their sides, stood on a table nearby. It was from these that my mother most often played and as a child I knew the Waldstein, the Appassionata, the Grand and the Moonlight as I knew the commonest hymn-tunes. Of Chopin she played chiefly the Nocturnes.

My mother played nearly always in the morning while my father was in London, but it was he who pressed her to play when guests were in the house in the evening, for he was touchingly proud of the ability which he knew, from information only, she possessed. There was never anything like an organised Musical Evening with instruments and music left in the cloakroom to be remembered in case of an invitation to play, but there was often music in the drawing-room which I heard from my bedroom above it.

The sterner critics of today would doubtless argue that the dwindling in numbers of amateur pianists that has come with the gramophone and radio makes for higher standards, that it is better for people who would never be very good performers anyway to listen instead of play, and that it is a pity I heard only my mother's playing instead of being able, as any modern child is, to hear great pianists at most times of the day. They may be right, and certainly informed musical taste is commoner now. But would I have heard those pianists if it had been an everyday possibility, if I had only to find the right station on the dial of a wireless set?

Would I have run in from the garden at the sound of music as I did for my mother's piano? Would I have lain awake at night to listen to a radio Symphony concert as I lay awake to hear my mother playing Schumann's *Carnaval* or a neighbour singing *Fly, white butterflies out to sea*? And if so, would I have felt the pride and pleasure which I always had at the sight of my mother actually making music?

[7]

Days at Wayside were of almost unbroken contentment for me, but only occasionally was one of egregious, ecstatic and memorable happiness.

I remember a day like that in the midsummer week of 1913 when I came from school on a Saturday morning to pass my tenth birthday at home. For a long time it had been a day marked out and ardently anticipated, and I woke to it, as one does to great days, conscious at once of its difference from all others, thrilled that it had come at last—almost incredibly after the impatient weeks. I went down to breakfast feeling one apart, knowing that, while all the boys around me would be learning arithmetic from Posh or Latin from Mr. Berkeley, would be grinding away at fractions or declensions in fear of 'notes', I should be on my way to Chipstead across the downs.

Before I had finished my roll and golden syrup, Mrs. B. called me up to the high table and told me not to go into class that morning, as a taxi was coming at half-past nine to take me home. A taxi! I had dared to dream only of a fly.

The craze that term was for photography. We all had little Brownie box cameras and took snaps of Mr. Alford and Mr. Townsend on the cricket field or more sycophantically of Mrs. B. in the rose garden. We would rinse our films in developing solution, dry them and put the one or two negatives which emerged satisfactorily from each into a printing frame in the sun. If this was not forgotten too long as, alas, was often the case, the printing paper behind it was put in hypo to fix the image, and we gazed with pride at the blurred result. Asked what I wanted for my birthday, I had written to say a daylight developer, a contrivance illustrated in Gamage's catalogue to obviate the need for a dark-room. I did not quite believe I should get it, for it cost a pound and my father was not a man to understand that the transitory desires of childhood are matters of life and death. But I sat in my taxi as it jolted down the chalky downland road and hoped with passion that it would be waiting for me.

It was. For once there were no qualifying clauses: 'You must take great care of it or it will be put away,' or anything but my father's 'Is this the thing you wanted?'

I could not wait to try it and used up a film in half an hour, calling the cook of the time to the back door to be photographed. Then I rushed up to the bathroom and followed the instructions to find that at least three of my six negatives had 'come out'.

But another present was a new grey flannel suit with long trousers and the pair of pale blue socks I had particularly wanted to go with it. As the Walter Smiths were coming to lunch, I could put these on.

I know that when any of us look back to childhood we find that, in memory at least, it was passed almost entirely in sunlight. Since statistics show no appreciable decrease in the annual hours of sunshine in England, I must assume that we idealise the weather of the past, conveniently forgetting the ugly days. But that day really was unclouded—I remember the sunlight on my father's straw-hat and on the Dorothy Perkins roses, I remember the sun-blinds drawn in the drawing-room to exclude it. It was unclouded in another sense. I was staying until Monday morning, so school was something infinitely remote. There was no shadow over the day.

My father went down to the station to meet the Walter Smiths and walk the half-mile back with them. They were living then at Epsom, a few miles away, but would walk to the station there, travel by train, walk up to our house and return by the same route. Walking was not considered the last resort of those who could not afford motor cars or an organised exercise to be indulged in by hiking clubs. It was a natural way to get from one place to another when, as usual, there was no hurry.

So we strolled back from the station past the chalky bank where wild convolvulus with its sickly-sweet scent grew among the bushes of wild roses. Then Big Sweetie and Little Sweetie refreshed themselves with a jug of claret-cup before lunch, and I was given a little because it was my birthday. I pretended I found nothing strange about the blue flowers of borage in the jug.

We had tea on the lawn, I remember, and there were more strawberries and cream than we could eat. The Rector, the genial Canon Stone, came and, seeing my new suit and flattened hair, called me a 'knut', the word of the moment for the overdressed. I was the only one of my generation present, a rare and happy experience for one of a large family.

That is the last I remember of that superlative day, though I expect I was allowed in to dinner at night. The group under the trees, the silver tea-tray brought out by the Mary or Martha of the moment, the women's large hats, Walter Smith's whisky-and-soda and cigar instead of tea, the easy chatter of the grown-ups, the brilliant garden behind, the happy complacence of it all. It was just fourteen months before the end of life as any of those grown-ups knew it.

[8]

I do not want to create spurious evidence in support of
Wordsworth's 'Child is father of the man', but it must have
been something more than chance that my first deliberate
act of rebellion was to maintain a friendship with the knife-
and-boot boy. I am no member of the Socialist Party, for it
has always seemed to me that Socialism should not consist
in stressing class distinctions by talking of the workers and
the bosses, but in first escaping all consciousness of those
distinctions in one's own mind, then fighting to eliminate
them whenever they appear. Coming from a background
like mine, to do this has meant being in revolt first against
parents, then against all the forces of precedent, education,
convention and respectability. Class unconsciousness has
brought more trouble into my life than anything else, but
what should I have expected of a creed like that? I do not in
the least regret it.

I should like to argue that my friendship with Beadle, the
knife-and-boot boy, was an early manifestation of it, but I
must own that it was in no way a conscious one. I simply
liked Beadle and that was all there was to it; my parents for-
bade me to associate with him and I continued secretly to
do so.

It was conceded by authority that Beadle was a very nice
knife-and-boot boy, the most industrious and the best-
mannered we had ever had. He looked, in fact, almost
angelic when he sang in the choir on Sundays, with his fair
hair and blue eyes and clean surplice. There was nothing
against Beadle, but it was not the proper thing, it was not
right, it would never do for me to go about with him. He
might use 'rough language'; I might pick up curious information. In any case, what would people say?

I knew by some half-formed instinct that he was a fine
boy, honourable, humorous, gay. He was older than I by

about four years, old enough to join up two years later and be killed on the Somme. He was generous and patient with a little boy's questions. So, unaware that I was showing the form of all my future life, unaware of any significance at all in what I did, I defied the ban imposed.

After all, how could my parents understand my frantic excitement in knowing that tomorrow Beadle was bringing his ferret to work so that I could examine this fabulous creature so often described in sagas of downland rabbiting? Or of my hearing, on Monday morning, the events of Beadle's one free day? Or of using his catapult? All these would have seemed to them unimportant compared with the impropriety of the friendship. So it remained clandestine and had the added fillip of all secret and illicit things.

CHAPTER XI

Things to Come

[1]

HOME WITH all its blisses was short-lived. There came inevitably the last week of the holidays, the last day, and the dreaded afternoon of returning to school. In the first few days of the term I would hear with wonder from other boys of parties and theatres they had attended, for most of them lived in London and none of their parents, apparently, had my father's conviction that theatres were 'full of all sorts of awful diseases'.

I do not think they were precocious little boys, or that at the time I was conscious of being more provincial than they, but to live in London and go to parties and theatres seemed to me for some years the last word in being sophisticated.

They brought back to school with them, too, remembered snatches of song. There was a ballad popular at the time with the plaintive words:

> 'Every day the people say
> There's a robbery in the park,
> So Mabel, dear, just listen here,
> I'm afraid to go home in the dark.'

Then in the big schoolroom, in the passages and dormitories of the school there began to be heard a different kind of song which persisted in the memory and could not be escaped for long. *Waiting for the Robert E. Lee* was the first I remember, then *Alexander's Ragtime Band* and, finally, maddeningly, ceaselessly repeating itself, *Everybody's Doin' It*.

'Everybody's doin' it,
Doin' it, doin' it . . .'

and so on almost without variation.

What we sounded, I suppose, when we sang those snatches, was the first welcome to ragtime, the first pipings of the age of jazz. The huge crescendo ahead, augmented by the gramophone and later by radio, would have seemed to us as unlikely as the prophetic drawings which appeared in magazines depicting the skies of the future, crowded with air traffic. But we did realise that there was something disturbing about ragtime, something different from all we knew of music. My mother's playing of Beethoven and Chopin, hymns in church, bands at the seaside and Mr. Gisby's dramatic singing-lessons were all I had heard when I began to chime in with the rest—

'Come on along, come on along,
It's the best band in the land!'

Or again and again repeated—

'Everybody's doin' it,
Doin' it, doin' it. . . .'

Thinking what has come of it all since then, how our lives have gone by to the ceaseless polyrhythms of jazz, how our years were haunted by the blues, how we knew 'cornet baby cries and laughing trombones', syncopated clatter, whining obscenity, harsh or melancholy beauty, how we welcomed the symphonic jazz of the 'twenties and more emphatically Negroid jazz of the 'thirties and the Swing music which followed and all the rising ocean swell which has overwhelmed and deafened us, I find it strange to remember that I knew a life without it, in which there were whole days with no music in them at all.

N

I want to make no prosy reflections on what has grown from the little bits of ragtime which came across the Atlantic then. (Such a harmless and amusing novelty, it was thought.) But when I remember that I am old enough to have known a jazzless England, to have heard in those scraps of noise and words brought back by boys to school after the holidays the first warning notes, I think that in nothing else is our life so changed in my half-century.

The 'dance craze' came while I was still at Rose Hill School and I remember on summer nights in the dormitory hearing from the Banstead village green the music of the local band. The school groundsman, who was a hero of mine, told me that it was he who looked after the big acetylene lamp by which the bandsmen played and held it on a pole while the villagers danced. Lying in bed, forgetting for a while Latin exercises, I would hear again *Alexander's Ragtime Band*, the music coming mysteriously up from behind the great chestnut trees beyond the school gardens. Dance music was no commonplace thing then and the thought of people dancing by lamplight on a village green a few hundred yards away was thrilling enough to keep us awake long after lights-out.

[2]

In another respect there has been little or no change in the preparatory school, I should like to bet, between 1910 and now—the observance of Sunday. Or has the Eton suit with its neck-scratching collar, kidney-freezing jacket and tight, uncomfortable trousers gone for ever?

We would dress ourselves in this already archaic costume and be inspected by Matron for clean finger-nails, tidily brushed hair and a general appearance which would do credit to the school when we attended the parish church. Then after breakfast we would gather in the big schoolroom and be issued with a double sheet of lined note-paper apiece, for it was time to write the weekly letter home. Those letters were for almost everyone the first original compositions achieved, though 'original' is scarcely the word for something which started always with the immemorial phrase, 'I hope you are quite well, I am.' Then? The essential stated, what embellishments were possible? One of the assistant masters would preside, Mr. Townsend or Mr. Alford, perhaps, glorious in the elegance of Sunday morning, and it was the custom for him to write on the blackboard a list of suggested topics. Thus the second sentence slowly scratched by forty or fifty pens would be—'On Saturday we played Cheam at home and won 2-1.' Next came a *cri de cœur* , the only quite spontaneous line in the letter. 'Please send me some tuck.'

For the rest we would return to the suggestions on the blackboard and perhaps become involved in something as long as this: 'Thursday was Mr. B.'s birthday and we had a half-holiday.' Or 'We break up on Friday next and I am looking forward to it.' Endearments other than the stern opening, 'Dear Father and Mother', and closing, 'Much love from your loving son', were not *comme il faut* and no attempt was made to show small boys how to communicate anything about themselves or their lives which could possibly interest their parents. In fact there was no communication, except in bare fact, and I do not suppose there is more today.

When letters were at last painfully finished, it was time to get ready for church, to take from one's desk a Book of Common Prayer and in winter put on the overcoat which covered the Eton suit. A pink cap with R.H.S. embroidered on it crowned this. We set off walking demurely, but not in a strict crocodile, for crocodiles were for girls' schools. The service seemed interminable, and, although the first thing we did when we had climbed into the oak pews was to look up the hymns whose numbers were prominently displayed, we never seemed to have any of the really rollicking or weepy ones which we liked.

After lunch was the school walk, a happy occasion with an illusion of freedom about it, for at least we left the confines of the school grounds.

It would be 'taken' by an assistant master, and if this was one of the more popular ones there would be a good deal of 'bagging' the right to walk with him. In this I did not join, because then as thereafter I have always felt an instinctive dislike of the whole cult of hero-worship when it is given to the successful, the charming and the glamorous. Mr. Alford and Mr. Townsend seemed no less dashing and remarkable to me than to the other small boys, but I did not share in the common wish to accord them devotion, as I have since not shared in hero-worship of generally popular figures. My admiration has always gone to the obscure rebels, the ungregarious and uncompromising, the outcast and the enemy of society who have the courage of their contempt for mass emotions. So it was the groundsman and remote M. Gazère who were my heroes at Rose Hill, not men of the facile charm of the young assistant masters adored by all. So in afterlife I have never worked up much enthusiasm for the naval and military heroes of the time, not even for Kitchener and Admiral Beatty in the First World War and certainly none for the highly publicised figures of the Second, like Montgomery. The airmen and airwomen of epic flights, Lindbergh and Amy Johnson, for instance, made me yawn, and names of sporting heroes like Bradman and Malcolm Campbell meant nothing to me. Left-wing poets and donnish novelists, radio comedians and guessing-game promoters, television singers and film stars may all be pleasant, hard-working people in themselves, but the hysterical admiration of them by both men and women makes me feel slightly sick. Give me someone anti-social, misunderstood or misunderstanding who finds himself sparring with humanity's shadow, give me a worker who strikes not because he is told to or as a matter of principle, but because he is just raw and sick at the conditions imposed on him, give me any man with the guts to assert himself against the herd and be trampled under their feet not for the sake of another party, another system, some footling theory or other, but because he does not like their bleat.

So I never 'bagged' a position on school walks near one of the heroes of the day but wandered off and was, for an hour or so, intensely happy. The road to the downs had only a few scattered houses along it, a pub and one or two cottages, and the autumnal trees of the Christmas term, the brilliant green of summer, were not marred by pylons, posters, garages, and the building estates which are spread over that same road now.

Freedom, on those walks, was relative, for it was forbidden to be out of sight of the master taking them, but walking with a friend, planning something which was to be a deep secret for all time between the two of us, talking ceaselessly, one had an exultant sense of emancipation. Mr. B.'s cane was forgotten—it was in any case a strict observer of the Sabbath and, although it could be promised for next day, it was remote and unreal as we came out on the bare hillside of the downs.

The white road, chalky and not well surfaced, has long disappeared among the villas, but when we took it then from the crest of the hill it descended, I could see my home. Once, even, the school walk met my parents, a cause of embarrassment more than of any less immediate emotion, for all the pink caps were raised and I had to be told by the assistant master in charge to go across and speak to them.

Tired and excited, full of plans and confidences, we returned to school for tea, and then came the hour in which we were supposed to read a set piece of Scripture and learn our Rep. The paragraphs we read were chosen the day

before, and on the Monday we were questioned on them
so that neglect of detail might mean a note to Mr. B. 'Who
was the wife of Zacharias?' 'What did he do in the temple?'
'Who appeared to him?' 'On which side of the altar was he
standing?' 'What did the angel say?' and so on. Perhaps one
had read those first verses of St. Luke's Gospel, but could
find no answers to the catechism, or perhaps one had not
forgotten the joys and plots of the school walk quickly
enough to concentrate. In that case there would be a note.
'Has not looked at his Scripture. S.A.' and the usual wait
at the study door.

Rep. was another matter.

'Winds of the World, give answer! They are whimpering to
    and fro
And what should they know of England who only England
    know?'

And what should we know of the meaning, the context or
the purpose of the words we committed to memory,
feverishly repeating them a hundred times till we felt sure
we could face Mr. Allen or Mr. Berkeley in the morning
and reel them off again? I can repeat all the lively and
musical words of that poem of Kipling's now, but perhaps
because I learnt to do so without understanding them, I
still do not know the meaning of two of its rhetorical
questions—

'Must we borrow a clout from the Boer—to plaster anew
    with dirt?
An Irish liar's bandage, or an English coward's shirt?'

A little less problematical were the words of another
Kipling poem we learnt—

'Kamal is out with twenty men to raise the Border side
And he has lifted the Colonel's mare that is the Colonel's
    pride.'

That was all right, but there was a shibboleth that came
first about East is East and West is West which nobody

understood and everyone could repeat as though they were mesmerised into making the correct sounds.

We sat for an hour in silence in the big schoolroom to read that Scripture and learn that Rep. What senseless tyranny it was to expect eight- and nine-year-old boys to sit still and concentrate on meaningless words for that interminable stretch of time. Surely this, at least, has gone from the curriculum of the modern preparatory school?

[3]

The happier events were nearly always those which broke routine, even if they were repeated at intervals. Once a week, for instance, in the summer term, the majority of boys were taken by hired bus to the public baths at Sutton. Swimming was an 'extra' and, because my entrance had been secured at a fee rather less than the highest charged, my father felt it would be tactless to allow me extras, so I never did five-finger exercises under Mr. Gisby or joined the excursions to Sutton. About half a dozen of us were left in the charge of one of the assistant masters for a couple of hours before breakfast, and because the occasion was extraordinary it was delightful. We were even allowed to walk up to the cricket field by the way reserved for parents and masters, a way through unfamiliar gardens of lawn and laurel.

Even illness was a welcome change. One illness of mine, a mere chill, I think, brought me a memorable experience, for I was alone in the sickroom with a boy called Wolfe-Barry and his grandfather came down to see him, a brisk, smiling bearded man who resembled somewhat the recently dead King Edward VII. He talked to his grandson and before leaving tipped him, then, seeing me in the other bed, came across, and, telling me to cheer up, gave me 5s. It was

Sir John Wolfe-Barry, the joint architect of Tower Bridge.

Once a year the hay was cut and we would help with the hay-making, or those of us who were not being coached at the nets for a match with a rival school. It was deliciously out of routine to scrape up the stray grass left by faster hay-makers, and once earned us a 'Thank You' from Mr. B. himself.

In one winter term the family of Archie Ghosal, of whom I remember only two beautiful women in *saris*, celebrated his birthday by bringing down to the school a professional entertainer. What enchantment was this! I see now a rather pasty-faced man at the piano in the dining-room, singing comic ballads interspersed with carefully selected stories, and doing a couple of conjuring tricks, but to me then it was all comedy and magic in one exhilarating hour. 'So the Vicar saw that the little girl's Teddy bear had the buttons of its eyes sewn on close together to give it a cross-eyed appearance. "And what do you call it?" he asked her. She said it was called Gladly. "Why is it called Gladly?" "Well, didn't you say in your sermon last Sunday—'Gladly my cross I'd bear?' " ' We laughed till the tears came and even Mrs. B. seemed to find it amusing as she sat with the Indian family. But that was 1912.

Whenever an aeroplane was heard we would rush out on the lawn in a body, at first even if class was in progress. The cry of 'Aeroplane!' would bring Mr. B. striding from his desk, and none of his assistants tried to hold us back from a sight of the new marvel. We were given a half-holiday to go out on Banstead Common to see the contestants in an air race, and among them we believed we could recognise the biplanes of Blériot, Louis Paulhan, Henri Farman, and the national hero, Claude Grahame-White.

Flying was discussed by us almost as often and as profoundly as cricket and the names of its heroes were as familiar to us as those of J. W. H. T. Douglas and C. B. Fry.

'Bet Grahame-White could beat Sopwith.' 'Bet he couldn't. Bet *no one* could beat Sopwith.'

For then as now the primary point of discussion in matters of aeronautics was speed.

We looked back as well as forward in our breaks with routine and once a year celebrated Guy Fawkes' Day. We like to be thought an unaccountable race, and it is certainly curious that while days recalling great victories or achievements in English history tend to be forgotten there should survive this rather silly celebration of a piece of successful police work, with its customary elements of treachery and falsehood. A subscription was raised annually from our pocket-money to buy fireworks, and on the night of November 5th we would be wrapped in scarves and overcoats and go out on the lawn to watch the assistant masters, lit by Catherine wheels, send up rockets. The finale was always a fire-balloon, which we watched till it was out of sight. Then we were shepherded back to our dormitories, our spirits returning to earth like the rockets we had seen.

A greater day for us all, one which was long anticipated and discussed, was Boat Race Day. Loyalties were divided by fashionable devotions. Mr. B. was known to be Oxford, but one or another of the younger masters might describe himself as Cambridge. 'Please, sir, are you Oxford or Cambridge?' we would ask Mr. Townsend or Mr. Alford a week before the contest, as we tried to decide on which side to cast the favour of our support.

From somewhere blue rosettes would appear, and it was a poor adherent who could not find at least a piece of dark or light blue ribbon.

When the day came everything was impregnated by its spirit of rivalry. There was even a certain tolerance shown for wandering wits and failure to concentrate on tenses and triangles. In the break one could hear the Cantabrians' jeering rhyme—

'Cambridge, Cambridge rowing on for ever,
Oxford in a match-box floating down the river.'

Or the Oxonians bitter—

'Oxford upstairs eating all the cakes,
Cambridge downstairs licking up the plates.'

When finally the result was announced the cheering of the
victors made the humiliation of the losers hard to bear.

[4]

But the greatest event of the school year was Sports Day,
for this alone brought all parents down to the school,
brought Admiral Robinson and General Davies, Dr.
Vosper from Devonshire and Sir Charles Allom, Dame
Clara Butt—for now her two sons were at the school—
and Elizabeth York Miller, and all the rich and notable
London shopkeepers to see their boys compete in one of
the races.

Heats had been worked out by the assistant masters in a
way that would exclude no boy from participation in
something, and leave no parent without a glimpse of his
son on the track. They had been run off during the preced-
ing days to leave for this a well-arranged programme, varied
and not overlong. The cricket field had unfamiliar lines
chalked out and hurdles set in position, while a pink flag
flew over the pavilion. All was 'special' and exciting.

When the assistant masters came on the field there was a
temptation to cheer each entry, each beautiful blazer and
straw-hat. Mr. Parker, it is true, looked rather everyday,
but then he held a starting-pistol, while Mr. Berkeley had a
stop-watch.

For the Sports Day of 1914 there were over 150 visitors.
We would wait near the gate of the cricket field, and as our

parents came in sight we went to them and led them in. The men wore rather race-going clothes, there were a good many grey top hats and shining white spats, while women that year seemed to set no limit to the elaborateness of their costume. Hats were enormous and dresses looked as though several different ones had been combined to make one.

I remember that crowd of parents, and my father and mother among them. Mrs. B. would pass graciously from one group to another. 'I should so much rather stay and talk with you,' she would say to each, 'but I *must* go and talk to these people who have just arrived.' She looked splendid, and used all her charm to effect. Then, the sports over, we led our parents down through the gardens to the dining-room, where Moss, the handsome young footman in livery, stood by a vast tea-urn flanked by neat housemaids. Soon the cups were brought and plates of pretty cakes circulated and chattering filled the room. Boys were not expected to eat the cakes—they would have their tea later—but they remained with their parents as these talked to one another.

It was always surprising to find which other parents one's own knew, those of rather odious boys were described by mine as 'delightful people' and those of a particular friend would probably be dismissed as common.

Then some favoured parent was asked to present the prizes, and the winners went up for their cups and we all cheered.

This must have been within two months of the declaration of war, two months before the end of the epoch. But as an occasion it seems to me to stand well for its time—the snobbery and decorum of it, the dressiness and invidiousness, the leisureliness and complacency. There was not a suggestion of a threat to the way of life these people knew, there was little talk of politics and none of events abroad. A warm Saturday in June, a school sports day and a gathering of middle-class parents was certainly not the occasion for any hint of doom.

Mrs. B. smiled proudly over the scene, for this was her success. The merely academic side of the business could be left to Mr. B., but it was for her to organise, to entertain, to reassure. She directed Moss to direct the housemaids towards empty cups, she turned to congratulate a boy standing with his parents, she swiftly broke up conversations between parents and assistant masters which seemed to be growing too intimate. She missed nothing and she remained cool and unhurrying. She looked over the room with the eye of an *entrepreneur* and knew that everything was all right.

It could never change. There would always be public schools, so that preparatory schools would always be necessary. There would always be nice people with enough money to send their sons to them. They would always gather in their beautiful ornate clothes on Sports Days to see their sons win little cups and look fit and happy. There would always be a footman in livery and servants to wait and cakes to supply. There would always be peace and prosperity, and people would always know their places, and England would be England for ever. It was all so nice.

CHAPTER XII
End of Play

[1]

THERE IS still a dormitory area called Chipstead, and it occupies the site of the place I knew, but that Chipstead with all its smug and pleasant life was destroyed in August 1914 as surely as if the Sarejevo bomb had been atomic and dropped on the village pump.

The school broke up on Saturday, August 1st, the day of the Chipstead Fête and Flower Show. It was also the day on which France decreed mobilisation, but that, of course, did not cloud it for me, or for any of the exhibitors of flowers and vegetables or the people who came to enjoy themselves on the little fairground.

I was to have lunch at the home of Eddie Campbell Cooper, for my father was Chairman of the Flower Show Committee and this was the busiest day of the year for him and my mother. I should see them later at the Fête and go home with them from there.

The Coopers lived in a house called the Old Rectory, which was hidden in woodland on the edge of the Shabden estate. I remember it as being an attractive place with fine mahogany furniture and old silver in a room which looked out on the woods. There was a tall father, a kindly, talkative, bespectacled mother and Eddie, who was a madcap, irresponsible boy often in trouble at school.

Once again it was a brilliantly sunny day—war always seems to have fine weather for its coming. We walked down to the Fête in the afternoon and there was not even the threat of a cloud to give us apprehensions in the only matter that concerned us then—the weather. The field on which it was being held was already growing crowded. This field belonged to Mr. Cheeseman and was below his garden, so that from the Fête one looked up to the windows of his large white house crowning a gentle slope.

There was a brass band playing a march when I came to the field, but there was nothing in the least militaristic in the atmosphere. Whether war threatened or not, this was the year's great occasion in the village and everyone meant to make the best of it. There were two marquees for the exhibition of fruit, vegetables and flowers and for tea. There was a competition for ladies to arrange the flowers on a small table, and Eddie's mother had entered this and was extremely proud of her sweet peas and gypsophila in little silver vases.

The smell in the exhibition marquee was powerful but delicious, of grass under canvas, of flowers and fruit. People greeted one another with a special cordiality and the tall Rector stalked among them, smiling amiably.

At last I found my father and asked him for some money to spend on the swings. He gave it to me, but said I would do far better to spend it at the stalls and 'get something for it'. I entered a cake-guessing competition and had a shy at some coconuts—both in vain—and watched a man exhibiting the use of a potter's wheel.

Presently my father called me to go with him up to Mr. Cheeseman's house to tea, and unwillingly I left the stalls and competitions and went with him. I remember being in a very large room from which the crowd in the field was visible and one heard the noise of the band. There were several men there who kept talking about war and I was impatient to return to the Fête.

'It depends on Russia,' my father pronounced.

The words in his familiar, emphatic voice return to me

now, repeating themselves like the nightmare words in a film. It depends on Russia. It depends on Russia. That was August 1st, 1914.

[2]

When the Fête was over and my father had won a great many of the prizes for flowers and vegetables and the 'gentle-people' had returned to their houses, I went back to the field to see the dancing. It was dusk when I reached it, and I found that the band playing was from Banstead, the very band which played on the village green and was audible from my dormitory. What was more, holding the lantern on a pole, was my friend, the school groundsman.

I stood beside him talking for a long time. I was proud of my privileged position as a friend of the man who held the lamp and proud of the groundsman himself, who, I knew was a terrific slogger whose hard hitting I had backed in argument even against that of Mr. Allen. We talked of school and he gave me the startling information that Matron was not coming back next term, having fallen out with Mrs. B., that Mr. Parker went to the local public house and got a bit fuddled sometimes and that the Sergeant was not, in the groundsman's opinion, a sergeant at all. The groundsman doubted if he had even got to corporal.

The dancing went on; there were naphtha flares, while roundabouts and swings were doing a good deal of business with shrill girls and their young men. It was a warm August night and everybody seemed to be enjoying it.

The groundsman further told me, sacrilegiously, that he didn't think much of Mr. Berkeley as a cricketer and that Mr. and Mrs. B. were making a 'tidy bit' out of the school. Not once, though I stayed an hour beside him, did we mention the possibility of war. On the contrary, we spoke of something that had been amiss today, and the groundsman

said it would have to be different at next year's Flower
Show. Almost exactly a year later he was killed at Suvla Bay.

[3]

My father came to my bedroom one morning and told
me that Great Britain had declared war on Germany. Full
of the muddle of patriotic verse, impressive pictures of
battleships and world maps with large pink areas, I thought
this was an occasion for cheering. My father soon dis-
illusioned me. I was to think of war as a bad thing. When the
Stock Exchange remained closed for some months it was a
very bad thing indeed.

But, of course, I could not think of it as anything of the
sort. It was an exciting, new and glorious thing. Flags came
out in the village and everyone began to talk of beating the
Kaiser before Christmas. In the stuffy little village Post
Office run by two old sisters, cards of patriotic buttons
appeared, and in the windows of cottages were hung pictures of the King and Queen with tricolour edges or of
Lord Kitchener looking thoroughly master of the situation.

Eleven O'clock Service in the church on Sunday became
a changed thing, for very soon the Rector was reading out
a list, surprisingly long, we noticed with pride, of those
men of the village who were serving with His Majesty's
Forces. There was also the weekly spectacle of Colonel
Cochran, a white-moustached old man with a straight,
spare figure, ostentatiously rising to his feet and remaining
thus while the prayer for peace was being read.

Besides, I knew why we were bound to lick the Germans
and wondered how the Kaiser had the temerity to set his
forces against the British. (There were also the French,
Russians, Serbians, Belgians, Montenegrins and the rest,
but I did not even have to reckon them in when I made my

calculations of victory.) With all the peoples of the Empire on our side, with Canada, Australia, New Zealand, South Africa, India and the other Dominions and Colonies, it was clearly absurd for the Germans to have any hopes at all. Why, India alone could lick them—look at all the millions there.

Besides, had I not seen, almost learned by heart, a list of ships of the Royal Navy and known how it compared with the German? What about our Dreadnoughts? The Germans had not got any of them. We had forty-three battleships and eight battle cruisers and nearly twice as many destroyers as they had, moreover we had Admiral Jellicoe, who was the best admiral in the world. Anyone could see we should lick the Germans hollow.

Everything became patriotic. To be keen about the war, to carry little miniature flags of all the Allies on the front of your bicycle, to know the music of the Serbian and Belgian national anthems, to wear red, white and blue in some way, to display portraits of the King and Kitchener— this was patriotism. To feel the slightest doubt about almost instant victory was pessimism, if it was nothing worse. You had to be on the right side and be noisy about it, as though it were some gigantic Boat Race Day.

So to me, at eleven years old, it was exhilarating and quite unreal. Even after the first death of a lad from the village was reported—he was killed at Mons—it was impossible at my age not to feel that one was participating in something stirring, backing the right side, being patriotic.

[4]

Yet I doubt if the declaration of war that August meant as much to me as my first bicycle. It was a rackety old thing, a woman's model which my Aunt Fo-Fo had abandoned,

o

but it gave me a new heaven and a new earth. I learned to ride it in the orchard and was astounded to find how quickly I could balance for a few yards before falling sideways. Then suddenly there came confidence and I could ride about the orchard as I wanted. I decided to ride up the village street, and passed the Talbot Smiths' home, at which my father and mother were playing tennis. The sight of me riding by, before I was practised enough to leave the garden, did not even put them off their game, so safe were the Chipstead roads then.

I soon ranged wider. I would cycle to the top of Reigate Hill and sit watching the motor cars coming up, a very man-of-the-world occupation which would enable me next term to talk familiarly of Napiers, De Dion Boutons, Lanchesters, Humbers, Wolseleys and Sunbeams. I was even allowed to pack up my lunch and picnic in Reigate woods.

To me at eleven, who knew so little beyond his village and his school, it was with a swelling sense of adventure that I rode out each morning. But for the physical tiredness which cycling gave me I could not have slept at night, so impatient was I to ride again, to see new things, to cruise across the surrounding countryside as though it were an undiscovered continent. Not long ago to reach the black-smith's forge had meant a long and tiresome walk; now I could be there almost effortlessly in a few minutes and could stand and watch as I had always longed to do with no one to say, 'Come along now.' I could cycle to Kingswood, for so long a remote place known only by its name shouted after 'Chipstead' on Purley station, or by an occasional picnic there. I could ride down the Coulsdon road, passing the Scott-Wyllies' house, to see on my left the row of pine trees which had always held a mysterious appeal to me. I was scarcely at home all that summer holiday, for I could not bear to put the old bicycle away at night.

How inconstant we are to our pleasures. The collection

of birds' eggs which had meant everything that very spring
became a few cracked and battered shells in a cardboard box
full of sawdust, and the butterflies and moths of last summer
grew dusty on the top of the nursery cupboard. Even the
toolbox on which I had painted MUSEUM and which contained a number of curiosities collected through the years
by assiduous swopping and the generosity of grown-ups
was scarcely opened. My red and black Kaffir beans, my
stone from a goldfield in which a little gold was visible, my
pebble from the beach of Easter Island, my piece of coral
and my porcupine's quill were never looked at now. I
wanted only to ride from Wayside this way or that to see the
places which previously it had cost me so much effort
to see.

Sundays were infuriating, for I was not allowed to cycle
on that day. It was considered to be in bad taste to cycle to
church, and my parents, Sabbatarians more by inclination
than conviction, wanted nothing to disturb Sunday afternoons. But on Monday morning I would scarcely wait to
finish breakfast before I was away again.

I cycled over the routes of my walks with Miss Wain, but
with the infidelity of childhood I had forgotten her as I had
forgotten butterflies and birds' eggs. I did get off my bicycle
near Dr. Freshfield's house once in the vain hope that he
might walk by and recognise me and let me see those magic
rooms again. I could sail down the road to the station, passing the home of the terrifying bulldog without fear, since
at the worst I could flee his fangs by pedalling.

Then one evening, being near the church behind which
were a number of small cottages on the way to Coulsdon, I
met Beadle, the knife-and-boot boy, who was walking
home.

'Would you like to have a go on my bike?' I asked him,
and to the other joys of my friendship with Beadle was
added the unconscious one of patronage.

Of course he was longing to ride the bicycle—knife-and-boot boys in 1914 had not been given miniature bicycles at the age of three and subsequent ones of increasing size till they reached their motor cycle at sixteen, as are boys from homes like his today. He could ride—he had once ridden on his uncle's. Could he just go down the hill and back.

After that I would meet Beadle every evening as he left Wayside, and he or I would ride on the step while the other pedalled all the way to the church.

[5]

We did not go away that summer, for with the Stock Exchange closed my father could not afford a family holiday. His prosperity was eclipsed for years to come; indeed, it never returned on the scale it had been while we were at Chipstead. He had already begun to talk of leaving Wayside and moving to some place where education would be cheaper. He had four of us at boarding-schools at a total expense which had not mattered while prosperity lasted, but now must have seemed to him crippling.

But I did not mind there being no seaside holiday for I had my bicycle, and the Surrey downs themselves had become a new place. As for talk of economy and a closed Stock Exchange, it had no meaning for me. I think no child is aware of impending change and only believes in it when it happens. The war was something to give new colour to life, it could have unpleasant consequences.

When the village shop kept by the brothers Philips, and referred to by all classes as 'Philipses', raised certain prices, there was great indignation. They were 'taking advantage of the war' it was said and would drive us to deal with someone else. Why should prices rise because Belgium had been invaded by the German Army? Why should anything in

Chipstead be changed? No one realised yet that its foundations had begun to crumble.

[6]

I used to cycle every day with a boy called Sharp, who lived in one of the new villas near the station. It was the time of the German spy scare and evidence was being found everywhere of the existence and perfidy of secret agents. Harmless people were attacked with monstrous brutality by angry crowds, and the general hysteria was greater and more dangerous than in the Second World War. It was not surprising that Sharp and I should find our own traces of the work of spies. These were certain cabalistic paint-marks on some felled trees, doubtless intelligible to the woodman dealing with them, but highly suspicious to us.

I think it was I who first saw them as the work of German agents communicating with one another. Sharp at once agreed with me.

'Don't let's tell anyone,' I suggested, and he agreed.

We came every morning to see if any additions had been made and then conceived the bold idea of watching the trees by night. This was never fully realised, as both of us had to be home by eight o'clock at the latest, but we did spend an uncomfortable half-hour with our bicycles hidden in a coppice nearby peering at the harmless paint-marks, yearning to see a tall, bearded stranger, probably masked, go up and add a cypher to his message. Or perhaps, even better, it would be some inhabitant of Chipstead whom no one had yet suspected and we should be able to show him for what he was. It added immensely to the excitement of that holiday, which was already lively with recruiting, marching soldiers, talk of the Kaiser and Little Willie and boasting about the prompt elimination of the German Army.

What might have been a less harmless manifestation of the spy mania took place in my own home. We had living at Wayside a governess for my younger brothers, a rather attractive Welsh girl named Jones. Suspicion fell on her as a German spy for some curious reasons. She had been governess in a German family, and when she had first come, before the declaration of war, she had received letters from her late employers and charges, of whom she showed my parents photographs. Her pretty, sing-song Welsh voice could be considered a foreign accent and she admitted to speaking German. Worse than any of these was her insistence, a very natural one in a large household, that she should clean her own room in the morning so that she could *keep it locked* all day.

I do not know how far my parents were seriously affected by this nonsense or whether her leaving us, which took place before the end of the holidays, was at their wish or hers. I had enough security work to do with my paintmarks.

[7]

Every family in those early days of war wanted to boast of relatives with the forces. Until my elder brothers joined up two years later, our stock was not high. There was my uncle, the Army doctor, who was promoted to Colonel and brought to France from the East, but he was a doctor, and that was not dashing enough for me. His brother, the Johannesburg lawyer, gave more scope by getting a commission in the Transvaal Horse Artillery. One of the Crofts, whom I did not know, got an M.C. that autumn and several more enlisted. No Cooke was of the right age, or near enough to it.

The pride of Chipstead was young Captain Lendon, who had retired from the Army to start farming on the outskirts of the village and was called up at once. He and his wife had invited me in previous holidays to come to their farmhouse and eat huge teas and see the threshing or take part in hay-making. They were the most popular new residents in the village for many years. 'Delightful people' my father called them. We felt almost the pride of relatives in an officer important enough to be called up so promptly. It was not until October when I was back at school that he was killed in action.

[8]

As in the Second World War twenty-five years later we were slow to realise that the end had come. I remember being driven to the house of my Uncle Edward Taylor at Woldingham and finding it just as usual, its terraces and lily-ponds and nice, bright, commonplace inhabitants look-ing as though they would be there for ever. Later that after-noon I found my uncle handing tins of petrol down to Dench his chauffeur, who was storing them in a cellar under the summer-house.

What happened to that petrol I do not know, but before very long the car for which it was intended was comman-deered, the pleasant house let to Doris Keane, who was then making her spectacular and memorable appearance in *Romance*, my uncle was in the uniform of the V.T.C., and Dench the chauffeur was called up, sent overseas and killed. In my own home I think there was more realisation that things would never be the same again. This was partly economical, because we lived, I imagine, on a fairly narrow margin and the sudden stoppage of my father's source of income must have perturbed him a good deal and have been in itself a threat to our way of life.

The difference was most manifest in the tennis parties of that August and September. The more lavish kinds of catering disappeared, there were less guests, and the occasions, though never subdued, lacked the hilarity and spontaneity of last year's parties. Besides, people would talk about the war, not as I wanted to hear it discussed in terms of flags, sovereigns, national anthems and licking the Germans, but with each passing week more seriousness. They spoke of Liège and Verdun, of the Marne and the Aisne, of Heligoland and submarines, and instead of dismissing all German forces as goose-stepping, dressed-up and cowardly, they began to talk as though it might take some time to beat them after all.

What I wanted, like every small boy, were straight comparisons between Joffre and Moltke, Sir John French and Von Kluck, Jellicoe and Von Tirpitz, the British Navy with so many ships and the German with only so many, things which showed plainly that the German advance through Belgium was quite irrelevant to the issue. But as September advanced the guests at our tennis parties, resting in deckchairs after their games, seemed tediously and anxiously concerned with details. They did not laugh at the Kaiser and Little Willie nearly so much and the younger men began to talk of joining up.

[9]

I did not know that September was to be my last month at Chipstead, the last month of security and permanence that I was to have and it was as well so, for it would have shadowed its pleasures and excitements. We had been six years at Chipstead, the longest period ever spent in one place by my father or by me after him. This was long enough to have given me the illusion that our places of residence were permanent, our neighbours always to be our neighbours, our life to be based on a single home. My mother had almost forgotten the sudden alarms and moves of her early married life, but now she began to recognise the symptoms of restlessness in my father, remarks about the drains, the distance from the station, the inefficient train service, the cost of boarding-schools for all of us. She knew, though I did not, that the long respite from change was ending.

Yet I think I had some presentiment of it in the last week before I went back to school, for it had never been so hard to face the prospect of leaving my home, and I had never before so taunted myself by remembering that this or that was the last of the holidays, the last Thursday, the last Friday and so on, then the last game of tennis, the last bicycle ride and the last day.

My last evening in that other world is vivid to me now, not only in its circumstances, sights and sounds, but in its emotions. It was fine September weather, scarcely autumnal even; one felt that summer was over, but not that autumn had come. I had been to tea with Eddie Cooper, and just before dusk we went out into the fields behind his house and met the gamekeeper of the Shabden estate, who carried a gun. We sat down in the lush grass, already gathering dew, and talked till the light began to fade.

A hawk hovered over us and the gamekeeper told us of the habits of hawks. He was a friendly and informative man whom I had never met before. I wanted to spend many evenings with him and Eddie Cooper talking about birds, hearing how each of the animals on his gibbet-string had met its death, each stoat and weasel and rat. I wanted this holiday to go on for ever, this evening to last for eternity, so that I need never enter the big schoolroom of Rose Hill again.

I was almost tearfully conscious of fleeting time and lost opportunities, I felt self-pity and fear of an impending doom. The last evening of the summer holidays was always hard to bear, but this one had a choking sadness which I had never known before. Unconsciously I was clinging to what

I knew, holding on to the things and places I loved, fighting against the merciless march of progress. I talked of 'next hols', and the gamekeeper promised to take us with him on his rounds, but as always when I was going back to school I had no faith in any return from it. This time my scepticism was to be justified.

We left the gamekeeper at last and went in to the Coopers' charming home to drink sweet lemonade left for us on the dining-room table. Eddie and I were to share a taxi back to school tomorrow, for we were too old now to need parents to accompany us.

I rode home through the gathering dusk, past Shabden, the house in whose artificial moat I had once ploughed my way through a river of dead leaves, past the village smithy which was so soon to become a garage, past the village pump which is preserved as a curiosity today, past the pond long since filled in, past the White Hart and Philipses, then came for the last time to Wayside. I was to stay up to dinner, but this did not console me. The good days were all over and the future was a threatening one. I cried myself to sleep.

CHAPTER XIII

Into the Tunnel

[1]

On a morning soon after the beginning of term, classes were interrupted by a sound of marching men singing *It's a Long Way to Tipperary*. There was an immediate and spontaneous cessation of work.

'Soldiers!' we shouted. 'Soldiers!' The word ran through to the classrooms at the back of the house and brought Mr. Parker and Mr. Berkeley from their lairs.

We went out to the lawn in front of the main entrance and watched while the whole column passed. It seemed interminable. The men marched with rifles on shoulders and sang lustily. Now and again one would turn and shout something to our cheering group and raise a laugh from those near him, but for the most part they marched and sang and ignored us and the people gathered on the pavement. They seem in retrospect all to have had moustaches, and their knee-high puttees and peaked caps looked smart and warlike then.

The incident set the tone of that term. To the fifty boys from homes much like mine the war had come as it had to me—a novelty, a new interest, a thrill. It could not be otherwise in childhood. It was only after a year or two of its oppression ('You can't have that because of the war.' 'Certainly not. There's a war on.'), and the ceaseless stories of hell in the trenches, and the loss perhaps of an elder brother or father, that the war to young boys became more than an almighty football match between the nations, a match which we were jolly well going to win. That first term of wartime in a smug little preparatory school was one of cheering whenever soldiers marched or announcements of small successes were made, was a time of pumped-up emotions of patriotism, of flags and national anthems and portraits of Kitchener.

To me, some of the disadvantages of war were brought home when I learned on the first day that M. Gazère had been called up and was fighting with the French Army. It was not that I felt any anxiety for him, for at this time no one known to me had been killed, and I had been so taught to believe in British superiority that I could see our soldiers and our allies as heroes with bayonets, sticking terrified German infantry like pigs. No, it was a purely selfish thing. I liked M. Gazère and liked talking French to him. The hours I had spent stuttering French phrases in conversation with him were bringing their reward and I had really begun to express myself a little. Besides, this was my own private interest; no other boy thought M. Gazère anything but mildly 'decent', for he had none of the elegance or youth or athletic prowess of more heroic figures.

I had one consolation. Last term he had brought back to school the most wonderful model ship which he had made himself. It was not a galleon, but a three-masted schooner, a graceful thing done in exquisite detail. This was to be presented as a prize this Christmas, not to the boy with the most marks in French, but to the one who had made most effort to learn to speak it.

'C'est pour toi,' M. Gazère said quietly to me, and I knew I should take it home at Christmas.

Meanwhile M. Gazère had been replaced by a dark-skinned, tall man who spoke German better than French and was the first master at that school openly to have favourites.

Mr. Gisby had quite caught the spirit of the time.

Abandoning all part-songs and *Lohengrin*, he began to teach us two patriotic ditties of his own composition, one called *Tommy, Tommy Atkins* and the other, in justice to the Senior Service, about a midshipman named Perky. He waved and banged rather violently over these, for he wanted, he explained, far more expression put into them by everybody. But that was pardonable composer's pride.

He then went to Mr. B. and obtained an order that every boy in the school should, as Rep., learn the words of the *Marseillaise* in French. Mr. Gisby played this with great flair and we brought out our four-syllabled *patrie* to support the *Entente Cordiale*.

Patriotic, too, was Mr. Berkeley, who gave us as Rep. after we had learnt the *Marseillaise* a stirring poem printed as a tricolour-surrounded broadsheet. It was enjoying a great vogue that autumn and had been written, it was said with wonder, by a railway worker, a simple man previously unknown as a poet. It was called *The Day*. I quoted it in this context in my novel, *Fall of Man*, but I cannot resist recalling it here, so exactly does it reveal the spirit of the time.

> 'You have longed for The Day,
> You have wronged for The Day,
> And now The Day has come . . . '

began the first verse and the lines at least had for us the advantage of being easily committed to memory.

> 'You have lied for The Day,
> You have spied for The Day.'

began another. It was this one, I think, which had these gentle sentiments—

> 'Slayer of youth and age and prime
> Defenceless slain with never a crime
> You are steeped in blood as a hog in slime
> False friend and cowardly foe!'

It ended with a tremendous warning, the exact nature of which I forget. 'But, hark you, beast!' or something of the sort started the last stanza and the enemy was fairly told that he was not going to get away with it.

Mr. B.'s patriotism took another form. He talked a great deal about the war to the senior boys and introduced one of those large maps speckled with little flags which were so popular in both wars, though in the second they could be used only intermittently when there was a line discernible between the forces. From his conversation it was learned by the senior boys that Mr. B. was a pessimist. This was said with awe at first, for popular sentiment until then suggested that pessimism was almost unpatriotic. But if Mr. B. the lord and arbiter of our lives was pessimistic, then pessimism could only be a new form of patriotism.

'Antwerp,' said Mr. B. impressively when it fell, 'has always been called a pistol pointed at the heart of England.' We goggled dutifully at that, you may be sure. When the First Battle of Ypres was raging and the Prussian Guards had been thrown, everyone knew, against the English in vain, and we were all sure it was a glorious victory, Mr. B. shook his head and asked what was left now of our only trained army, the British Expeditionary Force? When we cheered the sinking of the *Emden*, obviously a terrific naval occasion, Mr. B. pointed out that the *Emden* had already sunk fifteen ships, and asked where our food was to come from if the Germans were as successful in European waters. Clearly Mr. B. was a terrible pessimist, but that had no effect on us who were still busy talking of licking the Germans and shooting the Kaiser and Little Willie. Mr. B.'s pessimism was an eccentricity, and only added to the general excitement over the fall of Tsingtau and the surrender of German New Guinea.

[2]

War and patriotism coloured everything that term, but in a purely superficial way. For me it was a time of intense interest and development. I had begun to read a good deal for my own amusement, taking whatever was available from the two shelves in the big schoolroom which were called the Library. *Fifty-two Stories of Adventure for Boys* was there, I remember, and Ballantyne, Rider Haggard, Talbot Baines Reed and, of course, G. A. Henty.

But the book I found there which delighted me most was written, I believe, by E. Phillips Oppenheim and was called *A Prince of Swindlers*. I had not yet heard of Raffles, and in any case would have preferred the smooth character I myself discovered lurking, most inappropriately, even dangerously, in the school library. My man's story is told by an ex-criminal who becomes his valet and with lively admiration watches his adventures. The 'prince' is a tremendous 'knut', the clothes he wears dazzle the ex-criminal and also the inhabitants of the Côte d'Azur, where the 'prince' is very much at home. He wanders about, handsome, elegant, cultured and popular, picking up here a £100,000, there a quarter of a million. Once he appeared before an American millionaire as a conjuror and for the purposes of his trick required the millionaire's signature. Who would have thought that what was signed was a cheque for a couple of £100,000, cleverly set between sheets of pasteboard and ready for the occasion? I read this stuff greedily and was desolate when my prince was eventually killed by a piece of superb marble statuary falling on his head.

There was not much time to read, though, except for the half-hour between tea and prep and the few minutes before 'lights out' in the dormitory. No attempt was made to guide our reading and the nearest we ever came to the contemporary or to anything more real and recognisable than *She*

was when Mr. Allen gave readings from *Stalky & Co.*
What we did learn that term was boxing. It was not, like
shooting and riding, an extra, but for us all a weekly sub-
stitute for prep. Perhaps Mr. B. had been infected with the
general spirit of pugnacity or perhaps the suggestion had
come from one of the more influential parents. We were
divided into groups of suitable ability with an assistant
master to each group and lammed one another more or less
enthusiastically. I was in Mr. B.'s own group and have had
cause to thank him more than once in the years since then
for teaching me to use a straight left.

[3]

With war Mr. B.'s enthusiasm for his cane was damped a
little; I think, perhaps, because the Common Entrance
Examination was becoming less competitive now. That
term seems almost leisurely compared with others and there
was time for many pursuits other than translating Julius
Caesar and crossing the *pons assinorum.*

I made a collection which I kept for many years of the
national anthems of all allies, in sheet music with English
words. What I wanted with all those dreary tunes and the
idiotically translated words I cannot imagine, but have them
I would, even an extraordinary piece of plainsong which, I
was told, was the Japanese national anthem. I remember
Graham Murdoch obtaining some of these for me and my
immense gratitude to him. I bound them together and
gloated over them, delighted with my trove.

I began, too, to make friends for the first time. Boys of
ten and less rarely have more than momentary alliances, to
be broken by a bell ringing or a blow struck. But at eleven
they begin usually to make friends of another kind, friends
with whom to walk and talk in preference to others, friends

in whom to confide and with whom to attempt a certain constancy.

There was a doctor's son called Cedric Prowse, the younger of two brothers, who was my age to a day. I cannot imagine why he should have allowed me to consider him a friend, for he had already begun a school career of great if conventional distinction both athletically and intellectually and was popular with both boys and masters. I met him later when he was School Captain at Tonbridge with Colours for both rugby and cricket, and even at Rose Hill this sort of success could have been predicted for him. My other friend was equally popular, but for humour and charm rather than proficiency at sport. His name was George Lazarus, and he had come to the school through my father's recommendation to his stockbroker father. He was a gay companion, a small, untidy boy who learnt lessons with enviable ease. With one of these the Sunday afternoon walk became a happier thing and I felt rather grown-up in their company, for although they were of my age they were Londoners who had seen a great deal more than I had.

[4]

There was to be a new departure this term to accord with the martial spirit of the times—a Gymnastic Display and Concert at half-term. The Sergeant started on the very first Monday of term to teach us to march in step round and round the gymnasium. At first there were several of us who could not keep step and march like all the rest, but the others slowly learnt to conform, until I was the only Ishmael left and the Sergeant shouted at me in desperation.

There was to be figure marching followed by displays by picked boys swinging Indian clubs, using dumb-bells and forming a group on the parallel bars, but the opening event

P

was to be a march round the big schoolroom by every boy in the school, an exhibition of military drill which the assembled parents would find touching and impressive.

When the Sergeant's display was over, Mr. Gisby's would begin and, standing in a graded group, we should sing the *Marseillaise* and Mr. Gisby's songs about Tommy, Tommy Atkins and Perky. Union Jacks would be draped around us, and portraits of the King and Queen, surrounded by gilt cardboard laurels, would hang in the big schoolroom. Finally, an appropriate and timely selection, General Davies would present the prizes.

Nothing like it had been attempted before, but the war called for special efforts and displays, and Mrs. B. was not going to allow Rose Hill to appear half-hearted about licking the Hun. She herself attended both the Sergeant's and Mr. Gisby's classes and made loftily persuasive efforts to get me to march like everyone else, but without much effect. Hers was the first of many failures by well-meaning people to do much the same thing.

So we marched round the gym again and again as though we were soldiers marching out against the Kaiser, while Mr. Gisby played military music to help us keep step. Very soldier-like and aggressive we felt, for this was almost taking part in the war. Then we watched with admiration while the chosen boys made their clever group on the parallel bars.

For me the Display itself was by no means a success, for two days before it Mrs. B. and the Sergeant, after consulting seriously together, told me I was not to join the opening march round; I should be the only boy in the school to remain in the gymnasium while it happened. Nearly thirty years later I went through the same experience at an Officers' Training School in India, when, for the sake of the necessary uniformity of motion, I was hidden away alone during a march past. In neither case did it do me any harm, though I remember the rather desolate moments alone in the gymnasium when Mr. Gisby's piano in the big schoolroom was audible and I knew that the rest of the boys were appearing before their parents, and imagined my own parents' consternation. But if the mind is for ever in revolt, how can the limbs conform?

However, I joined in Mr. Gisby's programme and sang the chorus about Perky, who was 'sure to win a mighty victor-ee!'

[5]

No sooner was the Gymnastic Display over than the exhibitionistic belligerence of the school sought other outlets, and it was decided that the senior boys should produce a slightly abridged version of the patriotic play, *An Englishman's Home*. There were disappearances into the gym at night, where Mr. Alford coached them and persuaded them to learn their lines. When it became known that real costumes were to be sent down from London and real greasepaint used, there was great excitement and boundless envy of the actors.

While rehearsals continued, the rest of us were held strictly to the changeless routine of lessons and punishments. I was often 'kept in' with two or three other boys while the school was at football. Some weary nonsense with Latin tenses or constructions had kept me in the little classroom next to Mr. B.'s study on one fine December afternoon, when the door was thrown open and Mrs. B. appeared. I have a very clear picture of her; unruffled and dignified in appearance, she yet had a tremor in her voice and in her manner the dramatic intensity of an actress speaking her best line.

'Boys,' she said, 'they're shelling Scarborough!'

Awed though I was by this startling news and Mrs. B.'s

way of delivering it, I must have seen in it a possible way to escape from the tearful agonies of Latin.

'Please, Mrs. Browning, may I go and tell the other boys?'

'Yes. Yes,' said Mrs. B., for we had not yet heard about creating alarm and despondency, and I ran from the room piping, 'They're shelling Scarborough!'

'Put your overcoat on!' called Mrs. B. after me, wrecking her lines for the sake of her school's health.

I had no idea where or what Scarborough was, for it was not one of the county towns committed to memory, and I was not very sure what shelling meant, though I had vague notions of torpedo-like objects going through the air. But I knew from Mrs. B.'s manner that I had something good, something startling in the way of news, something that would not fail in its effect.

It did not. It was nearly five minutes after I had stopped the first game that Mr. Allen, who was its referee and who had kept me in that day, asked about my imposition.

'Mrs. B. told me to come and tell what has happened.'

Used judiciously, Mrs. B.'s name would still any member of the staff, and it did not fail to do so now. How those young men must have feared and detested her cool dominion over their lives, what things they must have said about her in their common-room. But for me and many other boys who passed through the school she remains a woman of great sensibility and kindness, a snob, no doubt, an opportunist and an actress, but a woman who understood small boys better than any of the men about her and could inspire and charm them. 'Boys, they're shelling Scarborough,' she said and her voice chimes back to me now.

The events of that afternoon, and the accounts we read afterwards of 500 civilian casualties, seemed to make *An Englishman's Home* more dramatic and apt. If the Germans could shell us, why couldn't they invade us? We began to feel that we were in the front line with our marching and the play that was being prepared in which young Grünhold, in full-plated and plumed uniform, was to play a Uhlan officer eventually foiled.

[6]

But suddenly, before the production of *An Englishman's Home,* the school was split into two by a quarrel between two Sixth Form boys, Rickett and York-Miller.

This was no stage drama, no action in the remote, unreal theatre of war, but pulsating and present, a vital matter for everyone. No one knew the cause of the quarrel—all we knew was that we must be on one side or the other. Neutrality was odious and, worse, dull. The excitement of choosing one's hero was overwhelming. Was one to be a York-Millerite or a Rickettician? York-Miller was clever and popular and supported by my friends. Graham Murdoch was an ardent York-Millerite and suggested that I should join the faction.

While I was hesitating, there was a sudden shift of popular support to York-Miller which left Rickett with only one or two faithful followers. My way was clear.

'Rickett,' I said, approaching him in the big schoolroom, 'May I be a Rickettician?'

He accorded the favour and I was a very proud and happy boy to be one of so few who knew the joys of being against popular feeling. Unhappily, however, a few days later there was a *rapprochement* between the principals and my eager loyalty was required no more. I like to remember that in my first partisanship I instinctively sought the minority.

Then there was another astonishing event. We heard that Mr. Alford was leaving at the end of the term to join the Army. He already had a commission as a second lieutenant having been in the O.T.C. at Clifton. Senior boys, York-Miller and Rickett happily co-operating, came round with lists for our subscriptions to buy him a leaving present, and this was very much more interesting than a mere master's birthday. The present—*no one* was to know what it was; it was an *absolutely dead* secret—was to be handed to Mr. Alford after the production of *An Englishman's Home*, and we were impatient to reach that fateful night, which would come a few days before the end of the term.

[7]

Rivington's Latin Primer was the book we used and in it, as an example of some construction, was quoted the simple statement, *Verae amicitiae sempiternae sunt* (True friendships are everlasting). One evening in prep, bored with whatever I was supposed to be doing, I began to make up rhymed couplets to go with the four Latin words. They were of a banality which passed the idiotic and approached the drooling, but after the first one or two they began more or less erratically to scan.

'Right through our lives, whatever scene befall
Remember these few words so dear to one and all—
Verae amicitiae sempiternae sunt.'

What can have prompted me to do the considerable work of committing this to paper in my inky scrawl?

'And if a quarrel rise between two friends
Forget not these few words on which the world depends—
Verae amicitiae sempiternae sunt.'

I must have been risking a note to Mr. B. next day by shamefully neglecting whatever I had to do but I pushed on.

'And if a friend wish to become a foe
Just make it up, don't let your quarrel grow.'

How easy it was, three written already and prep not half over yet. I continued.

'But if a foe wish to become a friend,
Let it be so and make your quarrel end.
Verae amicitiae sempiternae sunt.'

It would seem that I had exhausted the transpositions and
now groped for a finale, something with a rhetorical touch
to wind the thing up. This is what I achieved:

'If every man in England thought this right,
There would be ne'er a quarrel, ne'er a fight!
Verae amicitiae sempiternae sunt.'

When I had completed this I handed it to Cedric Prowse,
who was sitting next to me. He read it through, then wrote,
'Show it to Mr. Allen afterwards.'

Mr. Allen was taking prep. By what chance was it that
the most intelligent member of the staff was on duty that
night? A ruthless note-sender and inculcator of facts and
dates, he was yet perhaps the only master who would
not have snubbed this piece of presumptuousness on the
part of an eleven-year-old boy in a way to ensure no
recurrence.

While the cocoa and bread-and-butter were being handed
out after prep, I went across to his desk.

'Please, sir, I've written a poem.'

He held his hand out and I gave him *Verae Amicitiae.* He
read and chuckled, but not unkindly.

'When did you write this?'

I had not anticipated that.

'This evening, sir.'

'In prep?'

'Yes, but I'd finished my Caesar.'

'We'll see about that tomorrow. I'm going to take this.'

'Oh, sir!'

'It's all right. I want to show it to Mr. B. I shan't say you
did it in prep.'

Was that piece of dialogue, I wonder, now responsible

for the whole course of my life, or would the devil have come out anyway, sooner or later? For within three days it was known throughout the school that I could write 'poetry' and I could not have stopped if I wanted.

'Go on. Write one about the war!' 'Write one about the school.'

The next effort I think was an interminable patriotic ballad with a chorus to it of which I remember only one stanza:

'And in the Middle Ages
When Britain fought with France
Our troops were just as gallant
And ready to advance!'

I was surprised and a little bewildered by the ease with which I wrote this stuff and enormously enjoyed the sweets of fame. York-Miller had a little Gamage's typewriting machine, the kind in which the letters were on a wheel which had to be turned till the letter you wanted was over the set space, then pressed. He volunteered to type my whole production, and I kept for many years the thin, creased, fading sheets 'printed by A. York-Miller'.

Then, full of the sickly sentiments of the time, the lush and the patriotic which mixed to make Tommy and his mother at home, the King and country for which he dies and the whole blubber of flag-waving and marching tunes one artificially emotional mix-up, I produced something very awful which had an instantaneous success.

'He has left his mother standing
Beside her cottage door,
Has crossed the seas, is fighting
'Mid the bloodshed and the gore.

'With the bullets whizzing round him,
Comrades falling far and near,
Yet he goes on fighting bravely
Without sorrow, without fear.

'Then he thinks of far-off England,
  Losing every thought of war,
Is his mother well and happy?
  Will he ever see her more?

'And when he himself is fallen
  He may lie in peace to rest,
For he knows he's done his duty,
  And he knows he's done his best!'

That really bowled them over at Rose Hill School in December, 1914, and there began those questions which writers have to suffer all their lives, but which at eleven made me feel very important. 'How do you do it?' 'Do you have to wait for inspiration?' 'When do you do your writing?'

I was lost. I never afterwards wanted to be anything but a writer—a poet, I think I said then. I had tasted fame and glory. Even the magnificent Lance Browning, the Headmaster's son, who was then staying at the school waiting for his commission, called me up and asked to see my 'poems', and I ran to fetch them from my desk. (Lance was killed a year later). Even Mr. Alford looked at them, and Mrs. B. told me they were really very good. It is as well that Mr. Gisby never set them to music.

I do not think all this produced the least outward change in me. I certainly hope I remained an inky schoolboy shouting '*Ego!*' when someone said '*Quis?*' or 'Bags I!' or 'Fain I!' when I wanted to obtain or avoid something, or 'Sucks to you!' to administer a snub. I do not think there was anything precocious or priggish about the effect on me of the strange discovery that I could string words together in metre. But it certainly caused a sensation in the school and made that term my most memorable.

[8]

The production of *An Englishman's Home* was a fiasco. The uniforms and costumes arrived, and very beautiful they looked, and there was even scenery to make one end of the gymnasium into the 'home'. But the actors were suddenly overcome, not so much by stage fright as by a fear of the sound of their voices, so that they seemed to us to speak in whispers. Mrs. B. was reputedly a remarkable actress who 'could have gone on the stage', but she had not been asked to produce the play and now stood at the back among the guests and called musically, 'Speak *up*, boys! Speak up!' This, of course, produced sheer panic, and carefully memorised lines were forgotten and Mr. Alford had to prompt again and again.

But nothing spoiled the scene after the play, which was the presentation to Mr. Alford of the school's parting gift. Only a few senior boys knew what it was, and when the great moment came and a magnificent sword was produced, the cheering was long and vigorous. A sword! For war when Mr. Alford was going to it seemed to us the kind of thing suggested by toy soldiers, Lancers and Dragoons, Hussars and Household Cavalry, an affair in which a sword would be a useful thing for hand-to-hand combat with a Uhlan officer, combat in which of course Mr. Alford would decapitate his opponent and take over the fort.

He made a little speech of thanks, very quietly and rather touchingly—for he was still a boy of twenty and had not much more idea of the realities of war (or of life, for that matter,) than we had. We cheered him again and again and felt more than ever that we were *in* it.

[9]

A week or two before the end of term I received a letter from my mother which startled but in no way dismayed me. There was no dismay then in the prospect of change, for one searched at once and instinctively for its compensations. We were leaving Wayside—in fact, most of the furniture had already gone to the farmhouse near Tonbridge in which we were to live. At the end of the term I was to leave Rose Hill and next term should go to Tonbridge School as a day-boy.

I loved my home and had never thought of leaving it, yet that was at once forgotten in the prospect of living in a farmhouse. I should be able to wander about the farm as I wanted, my mother said, and it was a large one.

As for going to a public school as young as I was, without having to take the Common Entrance Examination on which my life had been concentrated for four years, it was nothing short of miraculous. The school in which I was, and everything in its curriculum, was designed, not to prepare boys for a public school, not to give them the strength of character and courage to stand up to its early hardships and dangers, not to arm them against possible corruption, not even to give them a firm basis of knowledge from which their later education could grow, but to make sure that they would pass the examination and enter whatever public school their parents had chosen. Awful Examples were quoted who, like the lady in the contemporary music-hall song who wanted to go to Birmingham and was carried on to Crewe, had been entered for Charterhouse or Rugby and found themselves instead accepting a last-minute vacancy in one of the lesser Woodard schools.

Can it be wondered, therefore, that with boys actually sitting in Mr. Parker's classroom doing their Common Entrance Examination under supervision on the day my mother's letter arrived, its most important news seemed to me that I should not have to take the examination at all?

The next was certainly the farm. This had been a dream for years—not to live on a farm, I had never hoped for that, but to spend a holiday on one, as children so often did in children's books. I remember that on the white and sleepy road between Kingsgate and Broadstairs once, I found a pig-sty with an old sow and her litter in it and lost all sense of time as I watched them. I loved the cattle on the Lendons' farm and the good, healthy smell of cattle in their stalls. I loved to see animals fed and I had once been allowed to sit on the back of a cart-horse. Now I was going to live among these things. That, and escaping the examination, blinded me to everything else. I scarcely thought of Chipstead, and the regret I expressed at leaving Rose Hill can scarcely have been a sincere one.

I showed the letter to several boys and masters, and was congratulated on not having to take the Common Entrance.

Mr. B. had been at Tonbridge himself and a good many of the boys he prepared were entered for it. It was admitted that it was a 'jolly good school', and for me, of course, with the partisanship of a small boy, it became the best public school of all.

So my last weeks were spent in a curiously exalted state, I could write poetry, I was leaving, and I was going to Tonbridge without passing the Common Entrance. Never having distinguished myself at anything in the four years I had spent at Rose Hill, I found that being one apart was pleasant. Masters spoke to me in a new man-to-man way, for although I was only eleven I was in the same position as boys of thirteen who were leaving that term for other public schools.

But I suffered one injustice which has never ceased to rankle. When my parents had come down for the Gym Display they had been shown M. Gazère's model ship and told by Mrs. B. with a meaning smile that I had a good chance of winning it. I knew from M. Gazère that it was for me. His very conditions for its award assured this, for no other boy had ever tried to converse with him in French. But now it was announced that it was to be 'kept for another term', which would, of course, exclude me.

I detest the vice of self-pity and have scorned to indulge in it under any of the bludgeonings of Chance, yet I feel a wave of it now as I remember that model ship. It was the only prize I ever should have won in all my life, so far am I from the prize-winning type. I was cheated of it and I am angrier now, forty years later, than I was then. Then I resolved to write to M. Gazère and tell him about it. This I did, sending my letter to the address I had used in the holidays. I never received a reply, which is not surprising, as M. Gazère was killed in December, 1914.

But at the time the injustice was not often remembered, for there was so much else to think about, including the new 'poems' which everyone insisted I should write. Besides, I was going to live on a farm and go as a day-boy to Tonbridge School.

[10]

The happiness of breaking-up day was an altogether new one. Instead of going home across the downs with Eddie Cooper, I was to find my way alone by train to Tonbridge, once even having to change trains on the way. Then, because it was now known to be my last term, goodbyes were said with a fervency, part hypocritical but also part sincere, which gave them a special quality.

All the assistant masters said goodbye to me, even Posh. Each had something to say—'Good luck at Tonbridge.' 'Don't forget the present conditional of être'—and Mr. Berkeley, unexpectedly and thrillingly, 'Send me some of your poems for the Rose Hill Magazine.' Mr. and Mrs. B.

were gracious and Moss winked and said, 'Going myself. Joined the Army yesterday.' The groundsman had already left and had evidently been right about the Matron, for she had not returned this term. It was not the day for visits from either Mr. Gisby or the Sergeant, so I failed to bid them farewell, but to everyone else, particularly to my friends Cedric Prowse and George Lazarus, I did so heartily.

A cab took me to the station alone and I had done with Chipstead and Banstead and pre-war life on the Surrey downs for ever. I thought only of what awaited me, the farmhouse and Tonbridge School, not for a moment of what I was losing.

How little could I have assessed that. Not only the personal loss, but the loss to us all. We should gain too, no doubt, and many of us would gain immeasurably and rightly, but the losses would remain, the great and the small losses, the big things that do not matter and the little things that matter so much. We were entering the dark tunnel of 1914-18 in which all was dark and unsure, but when we emerged blinking in the light of peace, there were changes from the life I had known which make those years at Chipstead and Banstead seem like life in another period of history or in a remote foreign country.

In my own family my father was never again the gay, enthusiastic spendthrift and host of Wayside. The war did not subdue him or rob him of gusto, but it aged him and gave him the first of those anxieties which eventually killed him—anxieties imaginary and real about money, his home, his children, servants, education, health, the future, the thousand cares which crowd in on us all. So accustomed are most of us to them now that my father's falling before them will seem strange and uncharacteristic, but he was born and brought up in an age of security, when anxieties were limited to illnesses and bank failures, and he never learned to live on the lip of a volcano as we have done.

There would be no more tennis parties like those at Wayside. Perhaps now and again in after years there would be 'a few people in' for tennis, but the crowded dining-room, strawberries and cream on the lawn and drinks on the terrace for thirty people were things of the past, for where could you find servants to wash up after them and how could you afford to entertain like that, anyway? The whisky-and-soda which Big Sweetie drank instead of tea would become in itself part of an economic problem when wartime taxation had done its work with the price of liquor.

As for Boxing Day parties, there were not many of our future homes with a room large enough for them, and, anyway, there were the same objections to them as to tennis parties, they cost too much and would have caused any post-war servant who might have been persuaded or shanghaied into the house for a few weeks to pack and leave instantly. So Cookes and Taylors never met again, and after Christmas Day came a void for the rest of my childhood.

Gardens my father would go on making, gardens with rustic work and Dorothy Perkins ramblers—indeed, he was making such a garden when he died twenty-two years later. But never again as at Chipstead, where he had two acres and a pair of greenhouses and for most of the time two gardeners and a boy, where he grew rare and difficult things like melons and gloxinias under glass. Gardening everywhere changed after the war; on the large scale it grew constricted and less enterprising, but at the same time it was taken up practically by more and more people. Between the great garden which employed several men and the cottage garden cultivated by its owner, there sprang up thousands upon thousands of villa gardens, small but often beautiful and thoughtfully arranged. From that December my father's efforts had to be made within such limits and I would not again know the orchard, the rose-garden, the little lawn, the front lawn, the tennis lawn, the kitchen garden which I had so long taken for granted.

My Aunts Eirene and Xenia did not—indeed, could not—change, but as the world changed about them and the old ladies of my childhood changed into striding matrons with short hair and golf clubs, or sensible young grandmothers who liked going to a dance on Saturday night, or interesting hostesses with cleverly designed dresses who were seen in the stalls of a theatre looking no more than fifty, my aunts became noticeable anachronisms, tiresome old frumps. Their old-fashioned clothes and manners were accentuated by the new poverty of my Aunt Eirene and the frightened parsimony of my Aunt Xenia.

But the changes in my family were as nothing to the general changes that were perceptible at the far end of the tunnel of war. There, in that new England that awaited us, that land fit for heroes to live in, many things that I had known and some of them loved in childhood had disappeared utterly. No one who cannot remember a horse-drawn England can realise what it means to see the horse reduced to its triple function of today, a rich man's pleasure, a gipsy's capital and means of travelling, and a worker on old-fashioned farms. The horse was everywhere when I first looked around me, the sweet smell of his hide as one patted him, the kind, intelligent face, the jolly noise of his hoofs were everyday things. The blue-lined open fly in which we crossed the Surrey downs over chalky roads or in wet weather, with its black hood over us, went to the station, the milk-float in which the milkman sometimes took me on his rounds, the hansoms, the Victorias, the growlers, and four-wheelers of London, the haywains on which I clamboured on the Lendons' farm, the cheery little vehicles on the Chipstead roads, dog-carts, governess-carts and pony-traps, the brakes, wagonettes, landaus and coaches in which people drove to Epsom for the Derby, the broughams I saw on the front at St. Leonards-on-Sea, all these must now have been broken up. Their beautiful wheelwright's work and the exquisite painting on them, their brilliantly polished brass and varnish, their fine upholstery, all is long destroyed by fire or exposure. The little cockades which coachmen wore in their hats are probably collector's pieces and the brasses from the waggon-horses' harness adorn the saloon bars of newly reconstructed Elizabethan inns. The horse population of my childhood has sunk to a tiny proportion of its strength, and life's the poorer for it.

The motor car, on the other hand, when we emerged from shortage, took possession of the land, and we shall never again live in a country in which roads can be cycled over or walked on with any pleasure except by those odd and defiant people who bind themselves together in wheeled battalions to chance their lives and wreck their health by stooping over the handlebars of fast cycles and fighting their way through dust and petrol fumes, the insults of drivers and the agonies of secret fatigue, to spend an hour at some over-crowded resort. The motor car with the petrol pumps and poster-advertising it brings, the facility it gives to movement so that no mere journey or visit has the significance it once had, its speeding up of life and the ease with which it enables one to run up to London for a show, go in to town for the shopping, travel twenty or thirty miles to a party, quickly eliminated all our leisurely and not ungracious manner of life.

Then, before the war ended, domestic service had become a survival scarcely worth the maintenance. Food, when rationing at last was done, started to deteriorate towards its debased state of today, and a family like ours which stood out against food preserved by any artificial means was soon considered one of obstinate reactionaries.

More satisfactory still to the new intellectuals, the economists and theorists who grew clamorous after the war, was it to find that our class as a whole, the middle, or, if you wish to be flattering, the upper middle class, the professional class, never recovered its prosperity. Here and there when peace came there were 'new rich' families, here and there the once well-to-do retained some of what they had long held so lightly, but for the most part we were all a good deal poorer than in those days at Chipstead. We never recovered that with which we were born, the sense of having a right to prosperity. That may have been an excellent thing for the future of the country and the confounding of privilege, but it was somewhat baffling to survivals from another age like my father and mother, who had no reason to expect any reverse to their fortunes more lasting than one of my father's periodical bad times on the Stock Exchange.

Nor have we ever recovered our sense of security. Once we had seen our world blown up, how could we assume that any seemingly stable perch and circumstances would last another year? After six years at Wayside I had begun to think of it as a home, as once people thought of their houses, whether they lived in a country mansion or a cottage. It was a building in which to be born and die, in which to remember one's grandparents and see one's grandchildren. No move in the future was to surprise me, and I never again believed in the continuance of things as they were.

There would be no more freedom as we knew it then, for an insidious bitch called Dora was already conceived and is still living. The slow process of turning a country of free men and women, in which the rights of the individual were respected, into the regimented Welfare State of today was already begun.

So much else of that leisurely life disappeared before the next five years were over that men coming home from service in the East gaped incredulously at their new England. London changed its very face, its customs, its dress, its traffic and its spirit. The hansom cab was no more, except for a few relics in Piccadilly Circus to be hired by drunken undergraduates. The good little chop-shop and even the City grill made way for the all-pervading J. Lyons & Co., the top-hat, except for diplomats and a few racegoers, vanished, so did Parma violets in gentlemen's button-holes, boaters, most watch-chains and tie-pins, the smaller music-halls, and the remaining side-whiskers. (Beards clung on for a time until the game of 'Beaver' in 1922 killed them.) Sunday morning parade in the Park was lost to Privilege, and Rotten Row appropriated by any bounder who could afford to hire a horse. The telephone rasped in every home and soon the ominous first crystal radio sets appeared.

Of Chipstead, as I knew it, nothing but the shell was left. Never again in that or any other parish church in the country did a Sunday morning service bring in virtually the whole population, and in many villages on main roads the inhabitants were too busy dodging coastal traffic to get to church, while the noise of the internal combustion engine drowned the church-bells, so that the Rector became little more than the custodian of an ancient monument or the organiser of a youth club. Picnics such as we had were rendered impossible even if anyone had time for them, for all the 'nice places' were soon built over and Chipstead joined Banstead, a spawn of little villas, across the Surrey downs. The village policeman, instead of calling for a 'Dog's Nose' in the White Hart in the morning, learned to stand outside it at night sternly enforcing the latest licensing hours. Children's nurses and governesses became as rare as cooks and parlourmaids, and breakfast in the morning changed from an English institution to a hurried, unsociable occasion, after which, for the ladies of the house, there might be 'the washing up'.

If town and country changed, the seaside changed with them. My Auntie Annie, still entrenched in her Victorian home, survived through the good fortune of Emma's loyalty for another ten years. But what became of the broughams on the front, each smarter than the last with their coachmen and footmen in cockaded livery? Where were the strings of bath-chairs and the horse-drawn bathing-machines?

Then, too, the cinema ceased to be a fairground novelty and took over its buildings in every large or small town in the country, so that huge hoardings showed titanic faces close together and the names of Mary Pickford, Lilian Gish, and Charles Chaplin were not as the names of our own actors were, familiar and revered, but the names of stars, like the names of stars in the heavens, remote, wonderful yet known to us all.

There were still men of character, but instead of being accepted with their quirks and achievements, and their points of difference from the majority as 'the Emperor' and Dr. Freshfield and in a more superficial way Walter Smith and Mr. Gisby had been, they were called eccentrics. Aeroplanes ceased to be comets and wonders in the sky and became things in which actually to fly, not as heroic aeronauts, but as passengers.

Much of all this was for the good and much, I hope with my heart, a state of transition to something far better for mankind than we could dream of in our constricted, commonplace life. But much that disappeared was precious, much harmless and delightful. There was an honour and decency in English life then which cannot be found in the feverishly selfish and shoddy life of today. We were stuffy, complacent people, blind to the future, convincing ourselves of the rightness of things as they were, unaware or unheeding of the poverty near us, insular and nationally conceited, but we had freedom, we knew how to live and we enjoyed ourselves. How many of the inhabitants of Chipstead today would even wish to claim those things?

I know now, I think, why Lot's wife was forbidden to look back. That morning as I jolted out of the gates of Rose Hill and took the road away from Chipstead I was leaving one world for another, and the world I left would be destroyed behind me.